Smoky Mountain Folks
AND
Their Lore

BY
JOSEPH S. HALL
Formerly Collaborator

National Park Service

D1131526

H3

PUBLISHED IN COOPERATION WITH

GREAT SMOKY MOUNTAINS NATURAL HISTORY ASSOCIATION

Dedicated with affection to
my Mother,
lover of the homespun idiom
and a good story.

Designed and Lithographed By
NORMAN PRINTING CO.
ASHEVILLE, NORTH CAROLINA

CONTENTS

Dan Cable, a lifelong resident of Hazel Creek and a member of a famous bear-hunting family.

I
INTRODUCTION
A FURRINER IN THE MOUNTAINS

THIS booklet consists mainly of stories and word sketches of people that I met, places that I saw, and things that I learned about during my first visit to the Great Smoky Mountains in the summer of 1937. On a minor government appointment, I went about from one mountain farm to another, and from one cove or valley to another, getting accounts and stories from as many people as possible. The idea was to collect information on mountain dialect in the Smokies through conversation with the people, by hearing them describe old ways of life, recount memorable events of the past, and tell folk tales and tall tales, utter proverbial sayings, and the like. No time could be lost; before long, the last of the Smokies residents ("old residenters") would leave their homes to find new ones in neighboring valleys beyond the Park bounds, or up and down and far across the land.

The movement to establish Great Smoky Mountains National Park is well told in various government leaflets and in books. About 1926 the states of Tennessee and North Carolina, in accordance with acts of their legislatures, began to buy land for the creation of the Park. Some five thousand families were affected. By 1937, when about 1200 people still remained, there was concern that all of them might depart without leaving record of their speech or oral lore. It became my good fortune to collect what I could record of the old dialect, along with sayings, tales, and accounts of former times.

Mid-June of 1937 found me leaving the halls of graduate school and jogging southward on the Southern Railway. A preview of the scenic delights of the Smokies came as the train clicked along bright rails in southwest Virginia on into Tennessee's great valley. The gentle curves of distant green highlands were a welcome change from a large city's glaring, angular lines. At Knoxville I boarded a bus which would take me a distance of forty miles to Gatlinburg, in the heart of the Smokies. This lumbering old vehicle crossed the long bridge over the picturesque Tennessee River, traversed broad, flat bottom lands, bounced heavily around sharp turns along the Little Pigeon River, and finally hove into the bustling, tourist-happy resort center of Gatlinburg.

At the headquarters of the National Park in this town I was shown the practical problems of my job and directed to the nearby Civilian Conservation Corps camp for living accommodations.

The Civilian Conservation Corps was an organization of several hundred thousand young men, authorized by the Reforestation and Relief Act of 1933, with the purpose of employing jobless youths in the protection and improvement of the nation's 600 millions of acres of forested lands. Especial projects were reforestation, the improvement of timber stands, the construction of roads, trails, lookouts and communications systems, the suppression of fires, and the eradication of insect pests and diseases in forest areas. In the Great Smoky Mountains the Corps, in existence from about 1933 to 1941, constructed hundreds of miles of trails, established an extensive system of erosion control, reforested many barren areas, assisted Park personnel in technical and administrative work, and built a number of fire towers.

When my work got under way, the camp superintendent gave me daily transportation on the big stake-body trucks which took the CCC work crews out to their jobs of constructing roads and trails. On the way, I would get off at some isolated farm, or I would stop at a thicket-flanked creek and walk up a trail to some remote cabin. When I finished one area, I moved on to the next CCC camp. Sometimes I lived with mountain families.

Here I was a "furriner" in strange hills and "hollers," about to enter on one of the most rewarding periods of my life, a period of adventure and of great human interest, and of contribution, I hope, to the cause of preserving the oral lore of this region.

As one traveled in the Smokies in 1937 he found few mountain homes alike, except for the old one-room log cabins and the newer flimsy "boxed" houses. There was the run-down shack of an old bachelor or "widderman" (widower), who was "just a-groundhoggin' it" (barely getting by), and the modest but trim cabin of a young couple who were just beginning to make their way in the world, and the large comfortable two-story house in fertile bottom lands of a prosperous farm family. This was no "Tobacco Road" country. Intermixed, amidst the lush greenery, were dwellings of the poor and some well-to-do mountaineers, and all stages in between, and built accordingly.

On the hills and in the "hollers" I found people who, educated or uneducated, loved life amidst productive cornfields, rich grazing lands, and green mountains. These were a people who had never been worn thin by the tensions of city living. It was not that these people, even the few prosperous ones among them, had not known hard times. Most mountain families had worked hard for a living, or for a start to better living. But there was something relaxed and easy-going about them— perhaps the result of working with the soil, or perhaps of making things go through thick and thin, or perhaps of taking life as it comes. There was an interest in each other's welfare and in helping each other out— in work, in the pleasures of hoe-downs, music makin's, and corn-shuckin's, in sickness and distress. There was an interest that extended even to a stranger like me when people said from Cades Cove to Cataloochee: "Come in and set a spell," "Come in and have some dinner with us," "Come back and stay a week," and "Our latch-string is always out." How could anyone fail to like such "old-timey," "free-hearted" people? This is the way people must have lived in much of rural America before smart city ways began putting little walls between us.

This was a new view of American life for me. But times were already changing for Smokies people, as times had changed much earlier for people in less isolated areas. Such things as the National Park, a world war, large-scale industry, the automobile, and wide highways were driving into the realm of the distant past the "old residenters" with their interests in bear hunting, drying foods, plowing with oxen, and doing things in various antique ways. But more on mountain life in transition in a later section.

Visits to mountain cabins often took me on trails up creeks, amid the sound of rushing water with the fragrance of dank vegetation about me. Quiet "snake feeders" (dragon flies) poised gracefully over limpid eddies beside tumbling cataracts. Sometimes a small cloud of gnats hovered in the shade of alder trees along creek banks. Often, when the walk to a cabin through the mountain wilderness seemed endless, suddenly there appeared a clearing or a field of tall, leafy corn announcing that a house was near. Next might come a cluster of fruit trees and "bee-gums" (beehives made from sections of gum trees), and a kitchen garden with a paling fence around it. A pleasant voice from the porch might say, "Come up and get ye a cheer (chair)."

I enjoyed the relaxed manner of these people as we sat on the front porch on the characteristic split-bottom chairs exchanging news and views. The elderly told of old times or narrated their favorite tall tales with keen enthusiasm, or perhaps they described some unhappy event of the past.

In view of the increasing vogue of hill-billy songs, it was refreshing to come to know the genuine mountain music—the plaintive old ballads in strange modes, the lusty infectious music of the hoe-downs, the spirited singing of hymns old and new. It was a pleasure, too, to join in on the square dance and in the old tunes.

It was a novel experience to eat "cat heads" (biscuits) or corn pone three times a day, string beans always with pieces of "side meat" to bring out their flavor, "liver puddin'," or even fried chicken sometimes for breakfast, bread (biscuits) drenched in 'lasses (sorghum molasses) or "red-eye" gravy—and always strong coffee. A more unusual meal might include fried squirrel or groundhog or trout fresh from the creek, or even bear meat.

And there was always the dreamy mystery of haze-covered mountains, the wistful sadness of the songs and ballads, the grace and yet rugged abandon of the square dance, the rich imagination reflected in the mountaineers' speech and turns of phrase, and the gracious hospitality of these people.

7

All of this—coupled with lasting friendships—was a moving experience for me.

The following sketches represent the results of interviews and conversations conducted from the middle of June to the first of September in 1937. An exception is the final section on mountain speech, which is derived from all my visits to the Great Smokies, extending from 1937 to 1956. These accounts were originally written up as records of interviews covering whatever subjects the talk might touch upon. In this form they remain, substantially, although they have been grouped as far as possible according to general subject matter. Elderly people were selected as informants for the most part so as to provide authentic information on speech and ways of the past. To avoid needless embarrassment to family and kin, some names have been changed. The grouping of sketches and narratives may be seen in the table of contents.

An effort has been made to preserve the speakers' expressions as far as possible. Except for the introduction, words, phrases, and sentences in quotation marks are those of the speaker who gave the information.

The ages of people are those at the time of the interviews in 1937, unless otherwise specifically mentioned. It is safe to say that none of the original elderly informants are living today. Only a number of the middle-aged and younger speakers are now living.

There was certainly no desire to "make light" of the mountain people. Too many writers, knowingly or unknowingly, had done this before. As is well known, there are good and bad qualities in people everywhere. If there seems a tendency in these reports to disclose the odd aspects of Smokies life, it is because the informants themselves preferred to dwell on those details. It has been the desire all along to let the mountain people tell their own stories.

It must be explained that the stories and accounts contained herein are not set down as true history. Authenticated history was not the design of this series of sketches. It seemed desirable, rather, for the purpose of illustrating the language of the people, to write the stories as nearly as possible as they were told. Naturally, a critical comparison of accounts by different informants and a study of any extant documents are necessary steps to establish the true events.

II
"GIT OUT YER GUNS, BOYS, FER I'M BRINGIN'
A BEAR HOME ALIVE!"

Mountain Humor

The air was swarming with flies on the hot summer day when I sat on the porch of his cabin with Sherman Myers of Cades Cove. "Hit's a good thing, ye know, to put molasses on yer feet," he confided. "Hit keeps the flies off yer face."

One of his amusing stories had to do with the torrential rains or cloudbursts which frequently occur in the Great Smoky Mountains in the summertime. A certain Irishman prayed for rain, as a long dry spell had been killing his crops and livestock. "Lord," he cried, "if ye'll only send me twenty-five cents wuth of rain, that's all I'll ask fer." That night it rained so hard deep gullies were formed in his fields, and half the hillside was washed away. Surveying the scene of destruction the next morning, the farmer said, "If I'd a knowed that rain was that cheap, I'd a prayed fer only a nickel's wuth!"

Another story told by Myers does not reflect so much the mountaineer's sense of humor as his idea of what constituted a "big time." He described a bear hunt and the ensuing feast of bear-meat which Nathe Burchfield of Oldfield Gap, near Tapoca, North Carolina, and a group of his friends enjoyed. After a successful hunt, the party returned to Burchfield's cabin, "played the fiddle, danced, and drunk liquor until they had eat the bear up." All this kept them busy for several days.

The average hillsman found pleasure, not only in hunting itself, but in the reminiscences, stories and sometimes fanciful tales which grow out of it. Boyd McClure of Wears Valley, just outside the Park, related some tales of how a couple of bears were killed. One time his dogs had treed a bear after a strenuous chase, but he did not trust his marksmanship with his single remaining "cattridge." So he "clim" the tree "fer ninst" the place where the animal was clinging, and "onbeknownst" to the bear, prepared to shoot it. Changing his mind, however, he peered around the trunk of the tree and suddenly shouted, "What are you doing here?" Bruin was so surprised that he "let all holts loose, fell on a pine-knot and kilt hisse'f."

Obviously, not all the stories told by the mountaineers invite belief.

9

It is said that many tales are invented especially for the benefit of inquisitive "furriners." Boyd McClure was no doubt fabricating one of these when he told how "Panther Bill" Ramsey got his name. Ramsey, he said, was on his way back to the Russell Place (a hunting cabin which used to be on the top of the Big Smoky) after a day's fishing. He "lent" (leaned) down to get a mess of fish that he left in the creek when a panther darted out from a thicket and got him by the seat of the "britches." Not to be outdone by the animal, Ramsey jumped astride its back, "retched" around and killed him with his hunting knife.

Another time a man was "still-hunting"—that is, hunting without dogs—up a creek above camp when he caught sight of a bear through the underbrush. He fired at the animal, but merely wounded it. The bear, maddened by the injury, charged the hunter, who took to his heels. As he approached camp, he "hollered" out, "Git out yer guns, boys, fer I'm bringin' a bear home alive!"

Much of the humor of the mountaineer is concerned with the steepness of his hills. Three typical and current sayings illustrate this and also indicate the nature of the problems a farmer may have to solve to plant or harvest a crop:

> The hills of East Tennessee are so steep that the only way the mountain man can sow them is to stand upon an opposite hill and shoot the seed in with a shot-gun.

> Some mountaineers have to tie their growing pumpkins to stakes driven into the slope, so that they will not endanger the lives of people passing below.

> When potatoes are grown on a mountain side, the farmer does not need to gather them when they are ready for use; he merely puts sacks at the foot of the hill to catch them as they roll down.

Sayings about hillside farming carry over into other activities. For example, many a mountain family gets in its firewood by throwing it down the chimney.

Worm fence, eight rails high, in Cataloochee.

III
THEY COULD SHOOT A SQUIRREL'S EYE OUT
Five Smokies Hunters
TOM BARNES—THE "NOTED" BEAR HUNTER

Each section of the mountains seemed to have its celebrated character or hero about whom stories and legends were formed. He was usually extraordinary because of some quality or activity, but frequently strange and unusual incidents which originally had befallen others were attached to him. This process continued until he became more or less legendary. Stories about him were enlarged, modified, and embellished with imaginative details, and it was sometimes possible to see myths and legends in the actual process of development.

Such a celebrity was Tom Barnes, the "noted bear-hunter," who was born in 1818 and died a very old man. He lived in Barnes Valley, named from his family, which lies in the shadow of White Rock (now named Mt. Cammerer in honor of the late distinguished director of the National Park Service). The residents of this district were scattered among the neighboring hills of East Tennessee when it became a portion of the National Park. His son, Bill, ninety-four years of age when I interviewed him, lived in a substantial two-story house in the middle of his excellent farm lands at Hartford, several miles away. Bill, who took credit for ninety-one grandchildren, was deputy sheriff at the Crestmont Lumber Company on Big Creek, North Carolina, for many years. Tom Barnes also had a daughter living in Cosby section. Old Barnes' reputation, however, was by no means confined to the immediate area. Stories about him were zestfully told well across the mountains in Cataloochee. However, it is believed that the incidents here related of him were true. That he lived to a somewhat doting old age was suggested by his son's account of the twilight days of his life. At that time, for some reason or other, he had forsaken his family, as he had always done when he heard the call of the trail.

Tom Barnes had gone to Walnut Bottoms to live with Charlie Sutton and his wife. This change of residence was probably due to his desire to be near the wild life which he had always loved so much. At any rate, he made the poor old wife of Charlie Sutton carry his gun for him, for he hardly had the strength now to "tote" it himself. All day long, with the silent, patient woman near at hand, he lay watching for a squirrel or some other "varment." Bears, of course, couldn't be expected to come so near to a habitation during the day time. When he caught sight of a squirrel, he would take the gun and attempt to shoot it with an aim not so steady as it once had been. On one of his little rambles about the Bottoms, he came upon a deer with its legs caught in a hole. The old man didn't have his gun this time and was stalking about by himself; but anticipating the savor of roast venison, he lay down, determined to keep watch over the animal until a gun could be fetched.

Stories of his more robust years, as told by his son, do not reveal an ingenious hunter and game-stalker after the Indian fashion. He was not that kind of woodsman. He was rather, seemingly, an overgrown boy who wasn't happy unless he was in the woods, and to whom, consequently, family and farm were of no great concern. Bill Barnes told me how the "master hunter," as he called his father, killed a bear without a gun, a story which I had heard with variations from others. He was driving cattle one day when he came upon a group of men, bear-hunters, with a pack of dogs, who had cornered a bear, but were unable to kill him. The dogs were baiting the raging beast, barking and snapping at him, careful not to get in the way of his powerful paws or gnashing teeth. The men were standing safely to one side, cursing their misfortune in not having "a dust of powder" left. They had exhausted their supply in the strenuous but unprofitable hunt of the day. Tom Barnes, however, calmly advanced and proceeded to kill the bear with his hunting knife. He "stove" the instrument into the animal's stomach and cut a hole five or six inches across. The snarling beast was prevented from attacking his human assailant by the harassing dogs. This would have the appearance of a tall tale if it were not corroborated by such a trustworthy individual as Jake Sutton, formerly fire-guard in the National Park Service.

Bill Barnes went on to relate how Tom once discovered some bears in a corn field at Big Bend. He had a muzzle-loading gun with him and proceeded to make a gun trap. He cut a "forked stick" from the branch of a tree, cocked his gun, and braced the muzzle in the crotch, allowing the butt end to rest on the ground. He tied a long string to a tree directly in line with the sights of the rifle, tying the other end to the trigger. Then he joined some companions working in a neighboring field. After an uneasy lapse of time he heard a loud report, and shouting, "Boys, I've got him," he ran to his gun. Stretched before it lay a dying bear, which had ambled against the string, thereby setting off the fatal charge.

Tom Barnes was extremely fond of bear meat. While hunting with some companions one day, he decided that it would be best for them to scatter abroad to find their game. He caught sight of a bear at the foot of a hill. His son reported the incident thus: "He let drive at him, and the bear broke to run. Hit ran yan way up the mountain and

Bill Barnes, of Hartford, Tennessee, son of Tom Barnes, told stories of his father's bear hunts.

Barnes tuck out atter him. The bear was a-laying' down battin' his eyes when the master bear hunter found him. He shot him dead and cut him up into four quarters. He got two or three bullets out where the bear had been shot at by the others." By that time Tom's companions had arrived, and each of the four "toted" his share of the victim to the hunting cabin. They cut generous steaks from their portions, fixed them onto forked sticks, and roasted them over a blazing fire. Later, when they were all eating, the old man said, "Gintlemen, eat as much as ye can, fer you-uns will still be hongry for bear-meat in the morning." Despite the prolonged feast, each carried home seventy-five pounds of meat the next day.

"Uncle Tom got caught in a bear trap once," Bill Barnes related. "He had bought him some big new traps 'n had to have spring poles to set 'em with. One day a trap caught him—the teeth went right through his hand. He was fer up in the mountain and they was nobody to help him git it out. So he gathered up the trap with his hand in it and toted it. Directly he found a log layin' acrost a little holler. By standin' under it and bracin' his back agin' it, he prized (pried) the trap open. He helt one of the jaws down with his feet and raised t'other up with his free hand."

That Uncle Tom Barnes was a deft marksman is evident from the following story which Major Woody of Cataloochee told of him. He was once hunting in a river bottom when he saw a panther crossing the river on a fallen tree trunk. At the moment when he raised his gun to shoot it, he saw a bear following the panther and killed both.

THE INGENIOUS TOBE PHILLIPS

In this same mountain area, on Tobes Creek, lived a crafty hunter and trapper, Uncle Tobe Phillips, after whom the creek was named. His nephew, Jake Sutton, told of the clever manner in which Uncle Tobe killed a bear. He discovered a path which bears used between the "laurel slicks (rhododendron thickets) where they wallered," and their feeding grounds. It lay in the bottom of a gorge with sides so steep that the bears could not easily have scaled or descended them. The hunter knew that sooner or later, most probably that night, the animals would be crossing that path. Selecting a tree before which they must pass, he fastened a white handkerchief to its trunk about the height of a bear's head. Then, at some distance, he took up a position where he could plainly see the handkerchief and use it for a target. Bracing his gun in the crotch of a forked stick, he lay prone behind it. His wait was a long one, and the night was well advanced before his efforts were rewarded. Finally, however, he saw a dark object eclipse the bit of white on the tree and he "let drive." As the echoes of the shot faded away, he heard a shuffling noise in the brush, and then the groans of a wounded beast. Knowing that it was unsafe to approach injured

Bears, once hunted in strenuous "bear races", are now a favorite attraction for tourists

National Park Service

game in the dark, Phillips lay down to sleep until daylight. When it "began to break daylight" he roused himself and went to look for his victim, hopeful that he had wounded it fatally and that it had not wandered too far. His shot had been true. Near the tree in a thicket he found the bear stone dead.

"COON HUNTIN' IS BETTER THAN BEAR HUNTIN' "

Major Woody

One of the characters of the picturesque cove known as Cataloochee on the North Carolina side of the Park was Major Woody (Major was his given name). He presented an odd appearance in his bedraggled, worn-out clothes and his broken-down shoes. When he was a boy, he caught his feet in a threshing-machine, with the result that he was crippled. Even to his dying day he wore his right shoe on his left foot, a circumstance which gave an effect at once odd and pathetic. Although he was a born hunter, his lameness prevented him from taking part in the arduous exertions of bear hunting, which ordinarily required the combined labors of several men. He could not keep up with them on their long drives over rough country. "Besides," he pointed out, "there's more real sport in coon hunting. Hit takes only one man to coon-hunt, but when ye bear hunt ye've got to have a passel of men, some for the stands and some for the drive. When you tree a coon, you've got him, 'n there's a heap more hard work, 'n more slavish runnin' and trampin' in bear huntin' than in coon-huntin'."

Major Woody once saw three raccoons enter a hollow log. He crawled in after them and shone his light into their eyes as he prepared to shoot them. "They made fer me, and I twisted a right smart bit to keep them from biting me. Then two went out t'other end of the log, and I mashed the third one to death. Jonathan Woody got one, and the dog got t'other. The oil from coons is wuth more than lard and has 'most the same taste."

Like many mountain folk he felt that the Park "has rernt this country." "They have us hemmed in, 'n you cain't kill a thing. Over in Swain County a man named Calhoun was lawed fer killin' a bear that was breakin' into his chicken house. But Judge Webb told him to pertect what he had. The wust, sorriest things they is, like bob-cats, you cain't kill."

He told me that he used to kill bob cats by "breaking them down," that is, by breaking their backs. "I kilt five that-a-way." Game conditions in this area must have been very good in former times, for he said, "Mack Hannah, Mark's daddy, has kilt a sight of bear." And there was the testimony of Bill Barnes who used to hunt in Cataloochee when he was "just a chunk of a boy." Woody said that the best hunting grounds were "on the Balsam" (on Balsam Mountain), but that "some of that country is turrible rough."

"In bear hunting," he continued, "you usually go the day before and

Timber cruising party for the North Carolina Park Commission on the Great Smokies purchase in the late 1920's. George Stephens, long a lover of the park, is at lower right. George Stephens

find where the bears are a-usin' (staying). Ther's a bear waller in the swag under Spruce Mountain Tower." Hounds of the type locally known as "cold-trailers" are employed in the hunt. "They foller the scent and won't make any noise."

In order to have bear meat in the winter time, he told how on Cosby (Creek) and in Greenbrier (Cove) "they'd catch bear in traps, take 'em in, fatten 'em. They made cribs out a big logs 'n chained the bear to the crib. Hit takes a sight of feed to fatten 'em."

THE FAMOUS BLACK BILL WALKER

One warm summer morning I walked up a short trail from a point on Little River near Townsend, Tennessee, to Walkers Valley, a small valley enclosed by rather steep mountains. Here on the cool porch of a mountain cabin I talked with Ashley Moore, a pleasant middle-aged gentleman.

Ashley Moore told how Walkers Valley got its name, saying that his grandfather, "Black Bill" Walker, was the first man to settle there around 1865. "Some people named Webb came here from Maryville to have a summer school. They were the first to call it Walkers Valley." Moore was born in a log house on the same spot where his "boxed" house then stood. He had never been "out of sight" of the valley except for a six months' absence in the lowlands. For a living he "trapped for" coon and mink and said that his bees helped him out a "whole lot."

"My granddaddy was a noted hunter," he said. "He allus talked about his gun. He got over a hundred bear in his life and was such a good shot that he was ruled out of most of the shooting matches. He driv many a beef off on foot." He was referring to the practice of awarding cows as prizes in these contests. "Granddaddy allus kept bear meat in his smoke-house. Hit tastes like pork, and lots of people cain't tell it from pork. The fatter the meat is, the better."

Moore described a bear hunt at night that he took with "Black Bill." "We heerd a bear a-lappin' (tearing down branches of a tree to obtain fruit or nuts) and shined our light in his eyes. Then we tuck a bead right in his eye and shot him."

A story, which Ashley Moore told, may be fiction, but considering the famous hunter's reputation it is by no means improbable. "Black Bill" Walker and some others were hunting bear for a man who paid them by the day, and who made a business of selling the hides. One of the hunters had "hemmed" a bear when it suddenly eluded their guns by disappearing into a cave. It was a huge animal and the leader of the party was disappointed to see it escape him. He offered twenty-five dollars to anyone who would follow the bear into the cave and kill it. At first no one was willing to try, but finally Walker spoke up and said he would take a chance. The cave being deep and tortuous,

Bear trap of the dead-fall type near the top of Buck Knob. The heavy lid with pins projecting downward usually kept the bear from escaping once the trap had been sprung.

the hunter was in complete darkness, but he kept his gun in position ready to fire the moment he touched the bear. Sensing trouble, the animal suddenly "made a big noise like an old sow and started blowing slobbers." When Bill felt warm moisture on his face, he fired. He killed the beast but refused to give it up in exchange for the promised reward, knowing that its hide should be worth much more.

The narrator added some interesting details about his grandfather. "Black Bill was a good rassler too. They fit fair in them days. He kept good liquor and did a sight of bootlaggin'. Liquor used to be made in the slicks (rhododendron thickets). Later they made it in the flats. Some of the boys got twenty dollars a gallon for their stuff, but it sold fer as cheap as six dollars."

HOW "TURKEY GEORGE" PALMER GOT HIS NAME

The nicknames of some of the CCC enrollees attached to camps in the Great Smoky Mountains National Park were interesting for their imaginative color, and adolescent humor and irony. Among the few which I noted down were "Black Cat"; "T-Model," conferred upon a young man for his professed ability to "double-clutch" a Model-T Ford (rather hard to do if one remembers the shift on this vehicle); "Gater," so-called by his associates from Florida; "Little Bill"; "Dad"; "Windy Bill" (a boy who was said to tell "windy" tales); "Clum," a shortening of Columbus; "Hog Jaw"; "Cyclone"; and "Snake Eye." There was a vast gulf, however, which separated these adolescent names from such venerable titles as "Devil Sam" or "Turkey George."

"Why do they call him 'Turkey George'?" I asked Mrs. Lacky of Mt. Sterling when she mentioned him. "Hit's soze a body kin know him from 'Creek George' Palmer, I reckon," she replied. It was not until I arrived in Cataloochee that I heard the fantastic tale which explained, to the satisfaction of some, the reason for his unusual name. Uncle Levi Caldwell, the genial blacksmith of the Mt. Sterling CCC Side Camp in Cataloochee, told me how Palmer was once walking on the mountain without a gun and saw a "gang o' wild turkeys." He tried to catch one and chased it as it fluttered along. Finally he managed to grab hold of its legs, but as he did so, the turkey "riz" up into the air and carried him across a "swag" (gap) to the next mountain and courteously dropped him. After hearing this or similar accounts from several others, I was surprised, upon meeting the man himself, to find that so soft-spoken a person was the subject of such an extravagant story. He was about eighty years of age, and, with his wife, lived on a well-kept and prosperous little farm in Pretty Hollow. Now, of course, his neat acres belonged to the Park, although he and his wife were allowed to remain as long as they lived. Here they cultivated a portion of their original property and kept some livestock. He was strong, considering his age, and didn't mind working.

19

"Turkey George" Palmer of Cataloochee photographed at eighteen with his bear rifle, and at seventy when the Great Smokies became a National Park.   George Stephens

Asked how he had acquired his strange nickname, "Turkey George," he gave the following more credible account. "I had a patch of land in corn. The wild turkeys was about to eat it up, so I built a pen to try to catch 'em. The pen was ten foot each way, and I covered over the top. Then I cut a ditch and run it into the pen and covered the ditch over with bark. I scattered corn in the ditch so as to draw the turkeys into the pen. Next mornin' they was nine big gobblers inside, an' one outside. I stopped up the hole an' got me a stick to kill 'em with. When I got in the pen, they riz up an' mighty nigh killed me instead; so I got out and fetched a hoe. When they stuck their heads betwixt the slats I knocked them with it. After that I built about three pens in the mountains an' caught two or three turkeys. That's why they call me 'Turkey George,' I reckon."

Questioned about the activities of his youth, he said that he had made some money gathering and selling ginseng, commonly known as "seng" or "sang." Ginseng is an herb with an aromatic root which is highly prized by the Chinese in making medicines. "Ther used to be a good big scope of seng on the mountain. I could fill a tow-sack in half a day and sell it fer fifteen cents a pound green, or twenty-five dry. I raised seng, too—had a patch of it measurin' six by eighteen feet— an' made fifty or sixty dollars a season. Reagan had a store over in Catons Grove across the mountains in Tennessee. He bought our seng every fall."

"I follered huntin', too, an' set my traps in the spring but quit in July because the fur and the meat's no good at that time of year. Then I set 'em again in September when the mast (acorns, chestnuts, etc.) was good, and kept it up till Christmas. I finally went to cannin' up the extra bear meat we'd have. We'd sell it fer a dollar and a half a fruit jar. I'd get from three to six dollars fer the skin. It was eight an' a half foot long and about seven and a half foot wide. I still-hunted a good bit, too. When ye still-hunt ye take a gun along but no dogs. Fust ye find where the bears eat mast. They lay in the laurel of a day and have reg'lar trails but come out at night. I've done no trappin' since thirteen or fourteen years ago."

He went on to tell a little about early game conditions. "They used to be wolves in these mountains. They came right down in the settlement and killed sheep. Like fox, they're too smart to be trapped, so I went to poisonin' 'em with strychnine. I put poisoned sheep meat in bushel baskets an' took 'em back in the mountains. I went back some time later an' found two dead wolves."

Mr. Willis King, formerly Wildlife Technician of the National Park Service, as quoted in Laura Thornborough's book *The Great Smoky Mountains*, commented on the former presence of wolves and other wild animals in this area:

"The eastern woods buffalo, elk, the eastern timber wolf, the Carolina beaver, and the eastern mountain lion have disappeared completely. It is fortunate that the area became a national park when it did, because certain animals, such as the eastern black bear, the wild turkey, ruffed grouse and certain others, would have been doomed without government protection. A few white-tailed deer survived the thoughtless slaughter, but it is doubtful whether they can come back without importation of similar stock from the adjacent national forests. The eastern wild turkey, with protection, now appears to be past the critical point and on the upturn. This stock is probably as near pure as any today. But not until after years of rigid protection can the animal life of this region approximate the natural equilibrium which it had before interference by the white man."

IV
SOME PLACES AND PEOPLE

Much of the charm of the Great Smoky Mountains lies in the fact that every cove is different. There is considerable variation of scenic and atmospheric effect. Wears Valley (not in the Park) has graceful lines and gentle curves, with a dominant and harmonic climax in Cove Mountain. There is something precipitous and perpendicular about the Gatlinburg country, with its abrupt ascents to high mountains round about. Greenbrier is a wild, overgrown wilderness, with an almost tropical luxuriance of vegetation. Cataloochee has an appeal not easy to define, but one that probably has something to do with the steep, wooded slopes rising suddenly from a smooth valley floor, with its early morning splendor when fragments of clouds become tangled in the upland thickets; and with the majestic, ruffled surge of its river.

The beauty of Cades Cove is more complex. There again is the contrast of flat land and high mountains, but the effect is at once enhanced and tempered by the width and length of its level reaches, and by the noble sweep of its highland curves. The effect of both combined is quietly pastoral, yet powerfully moving. Unforgettable, too, are the clouds which from time to time gather about Thunderhead, presaging a storm by their black and purple undercoating, and their deep-pitched voices. "Hit's a-bilin' up thar on them mountains," said Aunt Becky Cable one summer's day when clouds were piled on the main ridge of Smoky. The sun elsewhere was shining brightly, and not a fleck of cloud was visible in the sky overhead. As often happens, the storm did not strike the lowlands, but the Gargantuan din above soon brought a reverberation in the suddenly rising creek, whose waters fairly fought to make themselves heard. Long after one has left the scene, he will retain a memory of the moonlit expanse of the fields on a clear night, or the sound of "music makin'" across the tranquil meadow in the gently settling dusk.

The creeks of the Cosby region in Tennessee, including Cosby itself, explained Tom Evans of Newport, were named by Uncle Tommy Webb, younger brother of Eli Webb, who was the first settler in that section. Indian Camp Creek, for example, was named from the Indian Camp built by Uncle Tommy at the head of the creek. A rock building covered with sod stands there still.

About 1880 Tom Webb made a business of packing liquor into the Indian Reservation and selling it. Liquor making, he said, began in earnest during the first world war. His guess was that he had made "two million" gallons in his time. The common practice then was to use fifty pounds of sugar for every bushel of meal and to "run it off" a dozen times or so.

Ramsey Cascades, the terminus of a trail which leads through a splendid unspoiled forest.

As a young man Tom Webb plowed his farm with steers, because horses were seldom used for plowing in those days. He also worked for sixty-five cents a day in a saw mill which stood at the site of the Cosby CCC Camp. Lumbering had begun on upper Cosby about 1875.

The first grist mill on Cosby was built by the father of Luke Shults and was in continuous operation as far back as Tom Webb could remember. Although it was once operated day and night for grinding rye, wheat and corn, it was later used but one day a week by its owner, Field Large.

The one-time thickly settled region of Cataloochee, North Carolina, has, like other such sections, Elkmont, the Sugarlands, Greenbrier, and upper Cosby, returned almost to its primitive state. The peculiar climatic conditions, including an abundant rainfall, in this region probably had much to do with its swift return to the wild.

The quiet, peaceful atmosphere which now pervades Cataloochee certainly carries no suggestion of the once turbulent times. The illegal manufacture of liquor was quite extensive in this area, especially during Prohibition days. Naturally, every stranger was under suspicion of being an officer of some kind. I was told that several shots were fired at the car of a ranger when the National Park Service was first established there. In those days it was supposed that every government car was driven by a United States Marshal.

"There used to be a mean bunch in Catalooch'," attested an informant of Ravensford, "an' Zeke was the meanest of the lot. He burned Creek George's barn an' cut the years (ears) off a man named Miles. Zeke was awful bad to drink."

But if there was a "mean bunch" in Cataloochee, there were also many honest and respectable people in that beautiful valley.

Ravensford, North Carolina, so John MacDonald, long a resident of that area, informed me, was so called since about 1920. Ravens Fork, he said, received its name from the great number of ravens in the region. (Paul M. Fink, in his booklet *The Names and Lore of the Great Smokies,* ascribes the origin to a former Indian chief called Raven, after whom an Indian village then existing was named.) There was a band mill in operation at Ravensford for a time.

Abraham Mingus, Dr. John Mingus' son, built a mill on Mingus Creek near Ravensford in 1887. This mill was restored in 1937, by the National Park Service, with the assistance of Aden Carver, a respected farmer, stone-cutter, carpenter, and miller of nearby Bradley Fork. Dr. John Mingus was one of the first settlers on the Oconaluftee. The earliest settlers came across Soco Mountain from Rutherford County, he believed. Jim Spillcorn had the oldest grant on Mingus Creek and obtained it by "entering" about 1805. "Entering" meant filing a land claim based on preemption rights. The creek was first called Spillcorn Creek. People "came to mill" from as far as twenty-

24

five and thirty miles away. A water turbine was installed about 1922.

GRANDMOTHER ENLOE OF TIGHT RUN

Mrs. Clem Enloe, an energetic and determined old woman of eighty-five years, was digging angle worms around her house when I arrived. She lived on Tight Run, a small stream or "drean" (drain) near Ravensford. She eyed my approach severely and cut short the banalities of introduction by exclaiming, "See that?" She pointed to a can half full of worms. "I use them for fishing, and I'm the only one in this Park who's allowed to." She was almost a legend now, so many tales had grown up around her relating to her encounters with Park Service officials about her supposed fishing rights. "I fish winter and summer," she added emphatically, implying that stringent Park regulations meant nothing to her. It was now generally agreed that she was harmless, though vociferous. Her chief interest in life was fishing. On almost any day she could be seen on the road with a string of fish in one hand, and her long pole in the other, or sitting in some shady spot with her line in the water.

A strange combination of qualities was Grandmother Enloe, as she was called by her neighbors. One moment she was explaining that she soon expected the call to eternal rest, even singing for my benefit a portion of a heavenly tune which she said she had heard the angels sing a night or two previously. The next moment she was cursing in vulgar terms the Swain County officials at Bryson City for not paying her enough relief money.

Induced to forego her fishing for one morning and to tell a little of her family history, as well as some of the events of her younger days, she led me into her living room and began: "My pa was William Connolly. He helped send off the Injuns to Arkansas. His pa gave him a piece of land on Shoal Creek, and he traded hit for some land here. My daddy come from Kentucky when he was a baby (about 1810).

"I had two brothers, Jess and Dee Connolly, who were in the War. They were on the Rebel side, and I'm a Rebel yit. Brother Dee had a Testament which he carried above his heart. Hit saved his life once when a bullet hit him.

"Colonel Thomas was the richest man in this country. He was chief over the Injuns. When my daddy was som'ers in the fifty (in the fifties) he went with Colonel Thomas to the top of Smoky to keep the Yankees back. But they come through here. I never saw the like of soldiers in my life. Every man had two hosses. Hit tuck from ten in the mornin' till late in the evenin' (afternoon) for 'em all to git through. They hit that river a-splungin'.

"Jeff Hughes built this place and sold it to Bob Burchfield. Bob Burchfield and Biny Enloe swapped places. The Enloes came from Rutherford County.

25

Grandmother Enloe loved to fish.

"During the War people had to go to Seviersville or to Augusty (Georgia) to get their provisions. They'd be gone nearly a month."

The story of Abraham Lincoln's supposed illegitimate birth, which was the subject of one of the University of North Carolina Folk Plays, was well known in the vicinity of Oconaluftee. In fact, there was said to be a strong resemblance betwen Lincoln and the Enloes, to whom he was believed to be related. According to Mrs. Enloe, Uncle Wes Enloe was Abraham Lincoln's true father. Uncle Wes lived "below the bridge at Ravensford in a house that has been gone a long time. . . . He took Nancy Hanks to Kentucky to have the baby and hit borned in Kentucky." Mrs. Enloe knew no further details of this curious account. It is thus presumed that Lincoln acquired his given name from Abe Enloe, Wes's brother. Aden Carver, who also told the story, had it that Abe Enloe, and not Wes, was Lincoln's father.

Before I returned to photograph Grandmother Enloe, I was advised to take her a package of snuff. I was also warned that if she was in her worst mood, she would never consent to having her picture taken. However, she readily accepted my gift and showered me with praise, and in one of the pictures she smiled.

AUNT MARGARET PARTON OF COPELANDS CREEK

"I was seventy-three years old the thirteenth day of last Jinneway," stated Aunt Margaret Parton of Copelands Creek, Tennessee. "My family, the Morgans, settled on the Spring Branch of Copelands Creek. One of my grandpaws was part Black Dutch and part Irish. The other was full Dutch. My great-great-grandpaw and my granny on my mother's side come to this country from across the waters. The whole Morgan generation claimed to be half Indian and part Black Dutch. All the Morgans is dark-skinned." Just who the Black Dutch were originally seems to be a mystery, though the term is well-known in the mountains.

"When I was a little girl, we'd have to pick a pint of cottonseed before goin' to bed, while Mother 'ud set and cyard," she continued. "I went barefooted—never had shoes on my feet 'till I bought my first pair by sellin' chestnuts. When a big frost was on, or when come a big snow, I'd run from Mother's to the first house as hard as I could go."

Copelands Creek was a turbulent place when Aunt Margaret was a young woman. According to her, troubles were "caused by liquor and bad women." She told of a "bad woman" who was drinking liquor one night with some men in Sevierville. "She declared she was goin' to see Emerts Cove or hell, before day. She was up behint a man on a mule." On the way to Emerts Cove the mule slipped from the road, throwing both riders into the ice-covered creek where they drowned. "She saw torment, I reckon."

27

Although this account has the semblance of truth, it appears to bear some relationship to the old folk themes of the curse ending in death and of the results of defying the devil. In the Frank C. Brown collection of North Carolina folklore, one finds a tale which has some elements in common with the present one. It concerns a man who made a drunken boast that he would win a horse race or ride his horse to hell. In the race he was killed in an accident on a road, wet after a rain, and supposedly went to hell. Tales with popular themes such as this, as they travel about the country, become changed to suit local circumstances and people.

A secret band of men known as "White Caps," a hooded organization, was organized to put a stop to the evil doings on Copelands Creek. "But," Aunt Margaret added, "they got to be wuss than the other side was. They whipped and feathered the bad women and got to doin' all sorts of meanness. They poured tar between the straddle of one. I give her some grease to take the tar off of her. She didn't have more than half sense nohow. I didn't hold with no such whatever. They had to raise a army of 'Blue Bills' to git shed of them White Caps."

Plowing with oxen.

V

Two Typical Mountain Men and Their Stories
Aden Carver of Bradley Fork

Despite his ninety-one years, Aden Carver was strong and in good health when I "passed the time of day" with him at Bradley Fork not far from the Oconaluftee River in North Carolina one pleasant afternoon in late summer. Tall and white-haired, he presented a somewhat patriarchal appearance. He was active about his place, although he had a son and a young man from Emerts Cove across the mountain to help him out.

When I arrived at his home, he was sharpening a saw. He paid us a daily visit in the Smokemont CCC camp, and he sometimes joined a crew of the boys detailed to the Mingus Mill where restoration work was being done. In years past, when the mill was in operation, he had served as mechanic there, and his advice now guided the CCC crew in reconstructing the old building.

Questioned as to the place of his birth, he replied, "I'm in sight of my birth-right. My father once owned this land from the fork (between Bradley Fork and the top of the ridge). It was a log house that I was borned in." He explained that he had lived all his life in the immediate neighborhood except for a period of twenty-six years when he did some "milling" in Tennessee in Sevier, Knox and Cocke Counties. He boasted that in six months there he "superseded the foreman." He also ran a sawmill for a time.

Like many other mountain people whose lands were acquired for establishing the National Park, he bore a mild grudge. "They just condemned and sold me out," he complained. In some cases in which land was condemned by the state for purchase, injustices may have been done, and certain pieces of property may have been undervalued, but his case did not seem to be one of them. Many resented the intrusion of "furriners" and, of course, it is a fact that a portion of those dispossessed of their property were victims of unwise investments of the money paid for their land.

Nevertheless, a number of the local people have profited financially from the Park, and the states of Tennessee and North Carolina have benefited tremendously. The fact remains, however, that mountain folk are, in general, sedentary and home-loving, and the establishment of the National Park brought a measure of unhappiness.

Great numbers return for the homecomings held in each cove or district where a settlement once existed. These annual events draw many people from distant places. The good attendance attests their affection for their former homes. In Cades Cove a certain family re-

29

turned frequently, as often as every two or three weeks in the summertime, and sat on the site of their former mountain-side home, drinking water from the nearby spring and sometimes picnicking there.

As to matters of interest relative to the vicinity of Bradley Fork and the nearby Oconaluftee, old Aden Carver first told how cattle were marketed when he was young. "Bill Johnson from about Johnson City come in every year and bought cattle. By the time he got to Haywood County he had three or four hundred head. He drove 'em to Virginia, which took a week or ten days." Traveling was difficult then because "our bridges wasn't good."

The first settler on Bradley Fork was a man named Cornwell. "This land was all entered, and Floyd was the man who entered it," he said. "This section used to be Haywood County, then Jackson County, and now it's Swain County.

"My father came from Carter County, Tennessee, and my grandfather Bradley came from Rutherford, North Carolina." As for the Mingus who operated the well-known mill, he said, "Doc Mingus was from Dutch Bottom right in below Newport. He come here because of the game and fish."

"When I was a boy the woods was chuck full of deer, pant'er, and wolves." Asked if he had ever seen a panther, he replied, "A plagued pant'er run me from the top into the field once. The first I seed him, he was placin' his feet to jump on me. I had downhill and nothin' in the way! I've saw one or two since, but I haven't saw a pant'er's track or a deer's track in fifty year. When the deer went out, the pant'er and wolf had to go." It was interesting to get this opinion as to why the deer might have become extinct in the Great Smokies: "I allowed they might a tuck the Black Tongue and died, just like the cattle tuck it. There was no cure for it."

As we sat on the porch I looked about for the customary "bee-gums" which are usually near a mountain homestead. When I remarked about seeing none, he explained that the honey was not good in that district because the "bee has to go too fur to get his sweetnin'."

With reference to the making of liquor before the Park era, he said, "Used to be every man had it in his home. You never saw a drunk man. I don't foller drinkin' but I've made liquor." He had had a sixty-gallon still, he said, and used to "run the beer" through it into a barrel. "You run it till ther's enough singlin's (first-run whiskey) to fill the still. The second time you run it through you get alckihol." Still-houses were built for the purpose of keeping the "beer" (fermenting mash) from freezing. His mother's name for such a still-house was the "Devil's Kitchen."

Aden Carver's daughter-in-law, a middle-aged woman at that time, was a Maples before her marriage, and was originally from the Greenbrier section across the mountain in Tennessee. Upon inquiry I learned

30

Many stills operated on Park lands were confiscated by rangers in the early years of the Park.

National Park Service

that there was a trail across the ridge by way of Richland Mountain, Dry Sluice Gap, and Porters Flat, a fact which helped to account for the intermarriage of a number of Emerts Cove and Greenbrier residents with those of Bradley Fork.

Like most women of the mountains, she willingly gave me some of her best remedies. "To break out the hives it's good to take some catnip tea. For blisters make a poultice of peach-tree bark." She followed this with a cure for the phthisic (asthma), which is similar to one used on Cosby Creek: "Take a sourwood limb; put it under the sill or under the doorsteps, and keep it until the child outgrows its measure." The limb, of course, should be cut to the afflicted child's height.

Another cure for the same ailment may be effected in this manner: "Take a lock out of the crown of its head, put it in a hole, and peg it up." Catnip and bone set may be used for colds. Bone set is "bitterer than quinine and hit'll kill ye or cure ye, one."

UNCLE DAVE SPARKS OF CADES COVE

In the midst of the beautiful region of Cades Cove, Tennessee, lived old Dave Sparks, seventy-five years of age when we talked together, known to his neighbors as Uncle Dave. Somewhat less idyllic aspects of the country were evident on the day we first met. It was shortly before noon; the sun was blazing in all its summer passion, and the air was still and sultry. Uncle Dave was faithfully cultivating his cornfield, "layin' by his crap" (hoeing the ground for the last time), and seemed glad to stop for a "spell" to talk with me, but not for long. A mountain man takes his work slowly, but seriously. He told me, however, that I could return the next day.

His mother, he said, was raised "over toward Maryville." His father came here from some "foreign country," but Dave had no idea which. In view of the unusual meaning which "foreign" (usually pronounced "furrin'") acquired in the mountains (that is, "distant," and not necessarily "across the ocean"), it was impossible to learn from him whether his father was an early immigrant to the United States or merely moved to Cades Cove from some other region like Virginia or South Carolina.

His father, Nate Sparks, was a "squire" (a county magistrate), a blacksmith, and a shoemaker as well. His mother used to weave the cloth for the family in the earlier years of her married life, and her old loom stayed in its place long after her death. Uncle Dave Sparks finally gave it to Mrs. Sims for display in her Mountaineer Museum at Gatlinburg, Tennessee.

At any rate, Uncle Dave said that he had some "kinfolks," the Moodys, over in Haywood County, North Carolina, and that two sisters of his father live there.

Uncle Dave went on to tell something of the conditions of living during his father's time. Before the whites entered Cades Cove (around 1800) many Indians lived here. Encounters between the local occupants and other Indian tribes, or perhaps with Whites, are evident from the numerous arrowheads found in the thickets.

When Sparks' father arrived, wages were twenty-five cents a day, and hogs sold for three cents a pound. Game was abundant, especially squirrels, deer and bear, "but there's hardly a deer in the mountains now," he added. (The fact is that, since early in the Park era, deer gradually increased and became very plentiful in Cades Cove). Sparks paused in his accounts to tell how a hunter of his acquaintance once found a wolf which had been caught in a bear trap. (This hunter

Uncle Dan Myers, a neighbor of Dave Sparks in Cades Cove, standing among his "bee gums".

called wolves "wild dogs.") Much stock-herding was done "on Smoky," and cabins known as the Hall (or Derrick) and the Spence cabins had been built there.

A hundred acres sold for a "hog-rifle gun and a little more." The value of such a gun, he said, was from five to fifteen dollars.

Men amused themselves with shooting matches, offering cows as prizes. The guns used, of course, were muzzle-loading and equipped with "caps" (percussion caps). In the early days when a person was "up agin' it" to start a fire, he would shoot a rag from his gun, the explosion igniting the cloth.

Uncle Dave Sparks' own experiences were by no means cast in the shade by those of his father. In the former's younger days he had "toted a Smith-and-*Weston* and killed two or three "bear" with it. He advised that in bear hunting one must keep to the lee of the animals "so they won't get wind of you." They live in "roughs" or "slicks" (laurel thickets) and have trails through them. When a bear is caught in a trap, he is prevented from dragging it off with him by its grab-chains, which anchor the trap to a tree or some other immovable object. A hunter must be careful not to approach a bear immediately after it has been trapped. At that time the bear is very dangerous and must be allowed to "quieten down."

For many years Uncle Dave kept cattle on top of the mountain, and spent much time there. "I've herded cattle plumb to Silers Meadows," he said. Sheep, hogs and horses, as well as cattle, were pastured in the vicinity of the Spence cabin. Hogs fattened on mast. They ate three kinds of acorns, those of the white oak, the chestnut oak, and, in the winter time, the bitter oak.

On the mountain top, there was also a small amount of farming. "I 'spect one time there was fifty acres there, under cultivation, that is." One of the cabins (the Hall or the Spence) "had a good barn until come a windstorm and blowed it down." The cattle lived on moun-tain "feeren" (fern), but often ate plants which made them sick. "When cattle eat colt's foot, they th'ow it up, and ivy (laurel) pizens them."

In his book, *Our Southern Highlanders,* Horace Kephart told of a late snowstorm "on the mountain" during which a number of cattle brought there for summer herding were frozen to death. I mentioned this account to Uncle Dave. "That was back a right smart bit," he said. "They was fifty-six head of cattle dead, all huddled up together. I seed 'em. It happened on the nineteenth of April, and hit was the latest snowstorm we ever had in this country. They froze at Spence Cabin, all together, in a place not bigger'n my house. When I saw 'em, the snow kivered 'em up." Asked if the storm had been very severe in the cove, he explained, "Snow is only shoe-mouth deep in the cove when hit's knee-deep on the mountain." Aunt Becky Cable, Cades Cove, ninety-four years of age, differed as to the date of the occurrence. She said the snowstorm happened on the nineteenth of May.

Uncle Dave Sparks mentioned the practice in the old days of using "oxens" for plowing. Uncle Dave had used them himself "when up agin' it." Once he had two yoke of oxens," but sometimes yoked a "hoss and a steer" together. He remembered seeing some women driv-ing "oxens" in a mill twenty-five "year" ago. On Tow String Creek, North Carolina, just outside the Park boundary, I watched an ox hitched to a sledge hauling a load of corn to the mill.

Before the National Park was established there was a large settle-ment in Cades Cove, and much "moonshine" liquor was made there. The distilling was done in the mountains and the "laurel slicks," where greater seclusion was to be found. "Just any amount of fellers packed

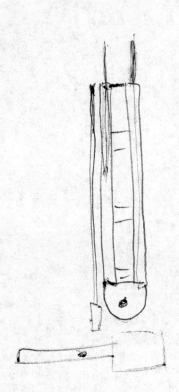

grain back there," recalled Uncle Dave, pointing to the wooded slopes. When asked if any revenue men had ever been killed by the moonshiners, as sometimes happened in other parts of the mountains, he replied, "I never heerd of a man gettin' shot nowhere. Bootleg, straight corn, sold for a dollar and a half to two dollars a jar" (probably a two-quart mason jar, the usual vessel in which liquor is sold in the Southern Mountains).

He then explained briefly how "moonshine" whiskey was manufactured. Liquor was made by mixing cornmeal and water, letting the "mash" "work" or ferment, adding sugar, "more sugar than corn," and then distilling. The liquor barrels must be smoked each time; otherwise they get "funk" (mouldy). A hundred fires could be seen on the hills at once in the old days. "The state officers were stricter than the revenue men, but the law never raided many times," Uncle Dave explained. One local resident, Tom Cooper, used to make stills, and Labe Myers, formerly the local National Park Service fire-guard, said that sheet copper, with which they were made, was procured from the mail-order houses. According to Tom Webb of Newport, Tennessee, large-scale liquor making began during World War I.

One of the colorful characters of Rebecca Cushman's sketches and portraits in verse, *Swing Your Mountain Gal,* the scene of which is laid on the North Carolina side of the Smokies, is Quill Rose, now dead. Uncle Dave told of him as follows: "Quill and his wife are buried at Townsend. Quill made a lot of liquor and drank a whole lot, but he had a good woman. He rode a little jack (jackass) with his Winchester on his arm; Quill was too lazy to walk. Quill lived over on Eagle Creek. He never had no family, but his brother Jake, he had a big family."

Uncle Dave chuckled at his memory of old Quill Rose riding his jack, with his "high-power" on his arm. Quill's capacity for whiskey was also attested by Boyd McClure of Wears Valley. He said, "I'll bet he has drunk this house full of liquor."

Next day, Uncle Dave conducted me to a low knoll not more than two hundred yards from the house in which he lived. It was the first graveyard of white settlers in the Cove. "John Cooper was the last to be buried here, and that must a been about 1905," he stated. A few "grave-rocks" lay round about, but they could not be distinguished from ordinary stones of the field. If they once bore inscriptions, nothing which resembled lettering was now visible. I carefully examined all the stones in the cemetery for information about the early mountain folks who rest there, but found nothing. The graves, he said, were four feet deep, or three feet down to the "box"; the coffins were made by hand.

Uncle Dave and Willie McCampbell once took a preacher and his sons to the top of Smoky for an outing of several days. They were

Making sorghum molasses provided excitement, novelty, and good times for family, friends, and neighbors. A shock of cane stands at the left. At the right is a mule pulling the large "lever" in a circle, thus operating the "mill", where a man feeds stalks into

rollers to press out the juice. The green liquid is boiled in the evaporator, center, until it turns a golden yellow in color. The wood is used for fuel in the evaporator.

National Park Service

slow in getting started from the cove, and it was late in the afternoon, or "evenin'," as the hillsman prefers to say, when they reached the ridge of the mountain. They were still "a right smart piece" from Spence cabin, where they counted on finding lodging, but being hungry, they decided to have a snack before proceeding. Storms descend suddenly upon the high mountains, and one was on its way as they were taking off their packs for a rest. Black clouds crept along the mountains and thunder boomed in the distance. "The storm scared us up," explained the old man, "so we told the preacher if he was goin' to ax a blessing he had to do it while we was gettin' the grub out. He went into it!" Uncle Dave told of the frequency of storms on Thunderhead, commenting, "Most every tree up thar has been strook by lightnin'."

In order to ascertain how far the speech of one section of the mountains has been affected by that of other sections, or other parts of the country, it was necessary to form at least a rough idea of the distance from home which people of that locality travelled. By questioning, the investigator soon learned that early in the Park era there was much movement about the Southern Appalachians, but very little beyond the mountains.

One young man in Emerts Cove had driven a truck in Middle Tennessee. A young woman had worked in the mills at Bristol, Virginia, on the Tennessee line, and had spent some time in eastern Kentucky. An elderly man had worked in the mines of Kentucky. One man's mother was now living in Virginia, and she made occasional visits to the Smokies. A young man from Cosby Creek was in Chillicothe, Ohio, serving a prison term imposed for "moonshining." An elderly couple had made a visit to California to see their daughter. A young couple had toured the North Carolina coast by automobile.

These latter cases were exceptions; the majority of those interviewed had never been out of the Southern Appalachians. In view of all this, it was interesting to know how far Uncle Dave Sparks had travelled from his home in Cades Cove. The longest trip he had ever taken was to Asheville, North Carolina, in direct line, about eighty miles. On other trips he had been "yon side of Knoxville," and to Robbinsville, Graham County, North Carolina, not more than twenty miles distant as the crow flies, but considerably farther by road.

VI

"THE WORST THING TO HAPPEN IN THESE MOUNTAINS"
THE FATE OF JASPER MELLINGER

"The worst thing to happen in these mountains, I reckon, was the death of Jasper Mellinger." This was the opinion of Zeb Lawson, fireguard in the National Park Service at Gatlinburg, Tennessee.

Mellinger, he told me, was accidentally caught in a bear trap set by John Beasly. In violation of the law, this trap had been placed in the middle of a trail without warning signs. It broke Mellinger's leg and held him prisoner for about five days before Beasly returned with his son to investigate his catch. Seeing that Mellinger was almost at the point of death from pain and exposure, and fearing the consequences of what he had done, Beasly ordered his son to kill the unfortunate man with a small log lying nearby. The boy, at first revolted by the idea, finally complied with his father's request. The two men placed Mellinger's body on a river bank and covered it with broken hemlocks. A few years later young Beasly fell mortally ill and on his deathbed confessed his crime.

Jim Cate, who lived on Little River above Elkmont, a point near which the death of Mellinger occurred, felt that Beasly was in no way responsible. Jim had talked to the detective who brought out Mellinger's bones, which were not discovered until three years after his death. Young Beasly's confession Jim regarded as just a story. There was no evidence, he explained further, that Mellinger had ever been caught in a bear trap, whereas it was highly possible that he had broken his leg by stumbling and died from exposure. Cate argued that the wound was too high on his leg to have been inflicted by a bear trap. He also pointed out that certain personal effects were found near the bones, including some money, a watch, and a rifle, and that John Beasly was too mean a man to leave these behind. A coroner's inquest was held at the scene of the death, but no true bill was issued by the grand jury. Apparently no circuit court trial was conducted.

Some time after hearing these accounts I struck up a conversation on the subject with a group of men who were lounging in one of the Lawson general stores in Wears Valley. I was told by a man who bore the name of Beasly, and who was related, presumably, to John Beasly, that the current story was false. He declared that it had been spread maliciously by enemies of the alleged murderer.

Reports of the inquest may no doubt be found in the local papers; but with the passing of time, such events are embellished with fancy in the popular mind, and become folklore.

Mellinger Death Ridge, a spur of Cold Spring Knob on top of Smoky near Miry Ridge, by its name bears silent witness to the tragic incident.

DEAD MAN'S CURVE

One of the stories told in the vicinity of Mount Sterling is, through its quality of horror, likely to become traditional. It tells of the dynamite explosion on Big Creek in Walnut Bottoms when the road was being constructed above the old Crestmont logging camp. This road is now used by the National Park Service for fire control. That respected old mountaineer, Jake Sutton, formerly a fire-guard, pointed out the spot as we drove over it. There is a huge rock cliff from which a passage has been blasted. This, he said, was Dead Man's Curve. This brief but pathetic tale explains the name (although one informant believed that the name already existed at the time, referring to a curve below this point where a man had been killed in a rail wreck).

There were six men at work on the blasting. They were laughing and joking in a pause from work as they passed a bottle of liquor from one to another. A hole had been drilled into the rock, and the dynamite was ready. Someone thrust into the opening a stick of powder, but it became "choked" (lodged) before reaching the bottom. When another worker tried forcing it with a crowbar, it exploded. Four of the men were blown to pieces.

Mrs. Neil Philips, formerly of Barnes Valley and later of Muddy Hollow, near Newport, Tennessee, told me how her sons returned from work on the road that evening of the disaster. "They jes' come in, drapped down in chairs, 'n' never said a word. I studied what was the matter." Mrs. Hardy Sutton of Chestnut Branch, Big Creek, said: "They was four got killed. I reckon Hardy holped pick up the pieces of their bodies."

Dogwood is at its best in late April.

VII

The Murderous Inn-Keepers, An Old Folk Tale
THE TALE OF ART FLOYD

One summer evening, following a clear day, storm clouds gathered swiftly and silently around Mount LeConte. When, with sudden vehemence, they discharged their watery burden, the accompanying din was greater than the crash of thunder.

The next day was bright and clear as the morning sun shone over the drenched wilderness. Since there was some talk around the CCC camp of trails having been washed out by the cloudburst, the superintendent decided it would be wise to have an inspection of the Appalachian trail between Newfound Gap and Dry Sluice Gap. Two foremen of the National Park Service were selected to go, and I was invited to make the trip with them. This was an ideal opportunity not only to traverse a portion of the Appalachian trail connecting Maine with Georgia, but also to accompany two mountain men whose families have assumed prominent roles in the taming of a wild country to the orderly purposes of men.

It was on that long tramp that I heard the strange tale here related, a story once accepted by not a few people as true. The narrator, Amos Wear, said it was so old that few now knew it. He heard it from his mother, although it was also told, he said, by Jim Floyd, the son of the leading character.

Many years ago, on the trail between Sevierville and Gatlinburg (there was no road then), some people named Black operated an inn and made a practice of robbing those who stayed for the night. Unaware of this, a certain Art Floyd stopped there one evening to take lodging. He was conducted to a room, and, as he was preparing to retire, noticed that the windows were barred. Thinking this somewhat strange, he went to the door and found it would not budge. He was pondering what to do when he smelled a nauseating odor, and after a search about the room, he discovered the body of a man underneath his bed. It appeared to have been lying there for several days and showed marks of a violent beating. At that moment voices in the hall were audible. The uneasy prisoner heard the words, "Let's get him good!"

Quickly he dragged the body out, put it in the bed, and covered it with the bed clothes. Then he so placed himself as to be concealed by the door when it was opened. Several men entered and set to hacking the body to pieces. Meanwhile, cautiously and unnoticed, Floyd slipped out of the room and fled from the place. At the nearest settlement he informed the "Law" of what was going on. Officers were dispatched to investigate. They arrived in time to arrest the murderers. A search of the premises revealed the graves of numerous other victims.

41

Later I mentioned this story to Sam Maples, a ninety-four year old veteran of the Union Army, who lived at the Gumstand. The Gumstand, a place on the road between Gatlinburg and Sevierville, was once a "stand" (near a gum tree) from which hunters shot game crossing Little Pigeon River. Well-acquainted with the folklore of the region, both he and the women folk of his household scoffed at the tale, claiming that without doubt it was circulated by some unsympathetic lowlander who found satisfaction in starting scandalous fictions about the mountain people.

That the tale enjoyed some currency, however, was revealed during a conversation with Jack Johnson, a resident of Dry Valley, Blount County, Tennessee, who, it was said, "can tell a great line of stories." Its quality as fiction was also brought to light, for the near-victim of his account was not Art Floyd, but Captain Fry; and the setting was elsewhere.

Captain Fry, he said, lived in Haywood County, North Carolina, just across the mountains. One day, astride an "old jack," he was driving stock to South Carolina, and he had occasion to stop at an inn. He was shown to a room in which he soon found himself locked. Noticing an odor, he found the stiff body of a man under the bed. Then he heard someone in the hall say, "Let's make it a sure lick this time!" Placing the body on the bed, he hid himself beneath the bed on the floor. Men entered, hacked the body, and one of them observed that it did not bleed. Fry managed to escape, got astride his jack, and was trying to urge the animal forward when he discoverd that its ankles were bound with silk thread. He dismounted, cut the threads and then hurried away to notify the "Law."

According to Fred W. Allsop in his *Folklore of Romantic Arkansas,* a variant of this tale known as "Murderer's Inn" occurs in that state. Like the present story, the Arkansas version seems to relate a real occurrence, but as the Arkansas collector suggests, it is probably old folklore material transformed to suit contemporary conditions and provided with local place and personal names. The occurrence of the same story in both the Southern Appalachians and the Ozarks is of interest in view of the fact that Tennessee was one of the chief sources of Arkansas' population.

VIII

"I'VE SPUN MANY A THREAD"

Some Accounts of Mountain Women

AUNT ZILPHIE SUTTON, GRANNYWOMAN

Chestnut Branch lies within the National Park near its northeastern corner. It has its source on the southeastern side of Mt. Cammerer and contributes its waters to Big Creek, which, in turn, carries them not more than a few miles to the Pigeon River. Before the Park era about nine families lived on the branch, according to Mrs. Zilphie Sutton. As for nearby Walnut Bottoms, she said, "It was thick of houses, thick of people up thar then." Only two families then remained. Mrs. Sutton, aged seventy at that time, recalled that White Rock (now Mt. Cammerer) was once known as "Old Mother," a name also applied to Chestnut Branch. When she was a girl, her family would eat wheat bread on Sundays, but corn bread and potatoes during the week. "I've sawed a many, a many hard day with my brother. I've grubbed, split rails, and built fence."

"The 'No-Fence Law' was the first thing that ruint this country," Mrs. Sutton declared. She explained that, even though the land was owned by a lumber company, hogs were once allowed to roam at will over the mountains. The free ranging of livestock, however, was brought to an end by the "No-Fence Law," the effect of which, contrary to the implication in the name, required the construction of fences by each land owner so that his stock might be confined to his own property.

The second thing was stopping folks from setting fire to the forest undergrowth. Mrs. Sutton described a strange method of combatting insects to which mountain people resorted in times past. "People burned out the brush every fall to keep out the insects," she said. "I've holped set fire and fight fire too. We never did see a beetle."

Asked if the local women made the cloth needed for the clothing of their families when she was a girl, she replied, "I've spun many a thread and wove many a cloth." "Linsey" she said, was used for underwear. To dye the cloth "we biled warnut (walnut) bark and put copperas in it." (She added that copperas was also given to hogs for the worms.) After showing me how the carding and batting of cotton is done, she boasted, "I can bat enough cotton in a day to quilt a quilt."

She talked spiritedly of her home remedies. Up to this point in my interview it had been difficult to find topics upon which she cared to speak freely, but here she began in earnest, describing first the medical uses to which a number of well-known mountain herbs were put. "Catnip is the best thing in the world fer a risin'. Make ye a poultice of it. An' the tea's good to cool ye down. Fever weed breaks the fever on a body. Bone set's good to break the fever and a bad cold.

Bread trays and gritters are made by hand. Ears of fresh or dried corn rubbed on the gritters make good cereal grits or meal for gritted bread.

National Park Service

Pink root's for worms   Birth-root's good blood medicine.   Indian physic tea is good to clean your stomach off.   Hit's good blood medicine, too."   Asked if she had taken much of it, she replied, "Lord, I've drunk a sight of it.   Whenever we'd get puny, mother would go to the woods, gather some yerbs, and make us some tea."

Mrs. Sutton described one method of treating a tooth-ache.   "You put a hole in a tree, say something, and get cured."   Unfortunately she did not remember the magic words which were supposed to effect the cure.

For the croup and the phthisic she advised, "Take a sourwood switch, make a mark on it even with the top of the child's head, lay it over the door, and let it stay there."

Further, Mrs. Sutton told of her experiences as a "granny woman" or mid wife: "I handled over two hundred babies," she declared. "I commenced when I was young.   I was long-headed—wasn't afraid of nothin'.   An' I never lost a woman in the whole boundary of 'em.

44

I've catched them (babies) here, in Sunburst and in Kentucky." Asked where in Kentucky she had been a granny woman, she said, "Middlesboro, on yan side of Cumberland Gap, where Kentucky and Buncombe County all jines together."

Actually, of course, Kentucky and North Carolina do not touch at all; Mrs. Sutton's conception of geography was somewhat hazy. Sunburst is a small town in Haywood County.

MRS. DEBBIE MATHIS OF MINGUS CREEK

Over on the North Carolina side of the Park, Mrs. Mathis was churning milk in a piggin, when I arrived following a two-mile walk up Mingus Creek. A piggin is a small bucket made of wooden staves, one or two of the staves serving as handles. She was a rugged type of mountain woman and not any too ready to talk with strangers. I did succeed, however, in getting some information from her.

Eighty years of age at the time of my visit, she "was borned at Ravensford" and her parents were born on "Luftee" (the Oconaluftee River). Among the first settlers of Mingus Creek were Sam Finney and Hosey Rough, she said.

Encouraged to talk a little about old times in this district, she began: "In the old days the chimleys of houses was made of wood and daubed with mud. When we needed thread to sew and weave with, we'd have to send to Knoxville and trade corn and chestnuts fer it. We also raised flax and, after separatin' the flax from the tow, made thread."

She described the four grades of flour. The poorest was the "brans," which were fed to cows and hogs. Next came "shorts," which were used "to make the best pancakes." The "seconds" and the "good flour" were used to make bread.

As to Civil War times she mentioned the practice of keeping "home guards" to protect the lives and the property of the local people. "Did you see any armies go through here?" I asked. "No," she replied, "we young-uns would shy (avoid) 'em." The Yankees once paid their house an unwelcome visit. "They just went in and sarched all over the house. Joel Connor and his wife buried their meat in the river bank so the Yankees couldn't find it." I asked her how many were in the raiding party. "They was a pretty smart gang of 'em," she replied.

Home medicine was practiced in her family when she was a girl, but if the nature of the illness warranted, Dr. Mingus was called in. "Dr. Mingus was a rale good doctor," she asserted.

It is notable that Mrs. Mathis expressed sentiments unfavorable to the Union. Similar feeling was expressed by others, for example, "Grandmother" Enloe, of Tight Run, Ravensford, North Carolina. The sympathies of the Smoky Mountain people were divided, the Tennesseans in general being pro-Union and the North Carolinians pro-Confederacy.

Mrs. Martha Jane Crisp's father's people lived in Graham County, North Carolina, and her mother's relatives in Henderson and Macon Counties. "I was borned and raised in Macon County, about fifty or sixty miles from here," said Mrs. Crisp, seventy-four years of age, a neighbor of Debbie Mathis on Mingus Creek.

When I asked her if she thought times had changed much since she was a girl, she replied that they had changed considerably for the worse. In her opinion, people had become more selfish and had little concern for those who were in trouble. "Why, in my raisin' up, two or three besides yer own would set up with sick people." The selfishness into which people had fallen, she prophesied, would not go unpunished. "We're livin' right in the eend (end) of time."

As to differences in clothing, she said that in former times jeans cloth was used by "men folks" and "linsey" for women's dresses. In jeans cloth the chain was woven of cotton and the filling of wool. "We dyed our wool with walnut roots, using indigo for blue and copperas for black." Maple bark yielded a purple dye, but only if the material to be colored was cotton. For green, hickory and alum were employed. In weaving, four treadles were required for jeans, but only two for linsey.

In the domain of cooking Mrs. Crisp described certain practices of her earlier years. Fruit and beans were dried for use during the winter. Apple butter, "punkin" butter, and sweet "tater" butter were favorites. Punkin butter was made by cooking the pumpkin, adding cane syrup, and then boiling it down. "After I was raised, I got to bleachin' apples. I never knowed nothin' about cannin' fruits and vegetables when I was a girl. I never knowed nothin' about lamps and lamp oils till I was grown." Sheep and mutton "taller" was used in the making of candles.

Like most women, she was not reluctant to tell her favorite remedies. "They never was but two doctors in my father's house," she proudly declared. To treat colds she preferred life-ever-lastin' tea; but if one suffered from catarrh, he must smoke the dried stalks and leaves of this plant. Catnip tea was likewise effective in the treatment of colds. "Hit's also good to make ye rest and sleep good." She used ground-ivy for kidney and bladder troubles. If one was attacked by "pneumonie fever," a strong tea made of black snake root and bone set would "break it up." For croup "take onions and fry 'em in grease and make a poultice and put it on the breast."

MRS. FLORENCE GASS OF RAVENS FORK

Mrs. Florence Gass was eighty years old when I interviewed her at Ravens Fork one morning. She first told of some of the early residents of the Ravensford district. The Gass family came there from Sevierville, Tennessee, about thirty years before. Rafe Hughes, she said, "lived by the forks of Ravens Fork and Tight Run." Ephraim Mingus, who lived in "the Big Cove," was her grandfather; she was a Conner before marriage. His brother, Dr. John Mingus, built the mill. Colonel William H. Thomas bought land from Ephraim for the Indians instead of taking land from them. All the lands on the creek are now "Indian Lands," except for fifty acres entered by Uncle Tom Bradley years ago and later owned by Bert Crisp.

As to Civil War times, she remembered the Yankees going up the road along "Luftee" (Oconaluftee) over the mountain to Tennessee. It took half a day for the army to pass. "The soldiers destroyed and stole a right smart. They stole horses, too. A great many (of the local people) took their horses out in the woods and hid 'em. The soldiers asked my mother to take off the piller cases and put meal in 'em."

Sturdy and respected mountain people, Mr. and Mrs. Will Palmer of Cataloochee, and their granddaughter Mary Alice Palmer.

"Old-timey" living conditions in the mountains are always of interest because of the trying circumstances the early people had to face. "Folks didn't know nothin' about cannin'. They dried fruit and beans. A whole lot of 'em dried punkin." This was done in a "dry kiln, made out of rock, with a shed over it, just like a molasses furnace." Most of the elderly women liked to speak of their weaving, although little weaving is now done except by those who are associated with the mountain craft industries. "The chain of our cloth," said Mrs. Gass, "was cotton, and the fillin' cotton or wool. My coverlid (bedspread) designs were the Irish Chain, the Double Rose and the Fan." Coverlids were made according to a "draft" or pattern. "You use three heddles for jeans cloth, two up and one down. This makes wool on the top sides. For linsey and blankets you have two heddles. Sometimes you use four or five for coverlids." Heddles are the levers or bars used for parting the threads to make the weaving design.

There was not much need for money in the mountains in former times. Her neighbor, Mrs. Enloe, had explained to me that during the Civil War the nearest stores were at Knoxville and Augusta, Georgia. "Once in a while a peddlar would come. He had a pack on his back and sold clothing mostly." Until fairly recent times many of the farms in the Great Smokies region were nearly self-sufficient, and goods and labor were exchanged. In a small grocery store near Cosby Creek I watched a woman barter chickens and eggs for flour and coffee. A little cash could be procured by picking berries and selling them to city dealers who make trips into the mountains, or by selling the surplus of a crop of beans. "In times gone by," Mrs. Gass continued, "people sold quite a lot o' cattle, too."

One of the curious place names in the region of the Oconaluftee is "Tow String Creek." Mrs. Fred Rolland resided on the creek in a house constructed partly of logs. This portion of the dwelling was said to have been built about 1850. "Every log in this place is poplar," she asserted. "They used to be a puncheon floor (made of split logs) in it, but my father tuck it up. The log section has pegs instead of nails, and the logs are chinked with mud. I know in reason the house was built by Uncle Tom Bradley. We had an heir in it, but we sold that to Bert Crisp." She was referring to the son of Mrs. Martha Jane Crisp of Mingus Creek. Of Uncle Tom Mrs. Gass said, "Bradley entered that land on Tow String Creek, I've heern." Asked to tell why the creek was so called, Mrs. Rolland said that it was named after an old Indian by the name of Toe who lived at the head of the creek. It has held the name for over a hundred years. She was unable to explain, however, how "String" became attached to the name. Mrs. Gass had a different explanation: "Two or three families lived on the creek. The men wore tow pants out a-sangin' (gathering ginseng). The pants shrunk up till they came up to their knees. People then got to callin' it Tow String Creek."

48

Aunt Margaret Packett of the Big Bend, a singer of the sorrowful ballad "Lord Thomas" and many other songs of the rich tradition of mountain ballad singing.

IX

"HIT'LL KILL YE OR CURE YE"
Mountain Beliefs and Remedies

Beliefs, both picturesque and practical, are common among the mountain folk. Corn planted in the "new of the moon" is supposed to grow tall and have spindly ears. To have your hands full when you first see the full moon means that you will have your hands full for a month. It is thought that you may get "dew-poisoning" if you walk through wet grass barefooted. St. John weeds wet with dew, Mrs. Vena Ramsey of Cosby Creek told me, will cause "sores and risin's" ("dew-poisoning") on the skin.

Mrs. Ramsey, sixty-seven when I first met her, is one who puts a horse-shoe in the fire to keep the hawks out of the chickens. Her daughter, thirty-two, scoffed at the notion that this precaution would produce the desired effect and referred jokingly to her mother's superstitious ideas and cures, such as this one for the croup and the phthisic. (These "cures" and other remedies similar to those given below were also recounted by a younger woman whose belief was somewhat wavering, for she said of them, in a tone of skepticism, "That's what folks around here believe.") Straighten a sourwood stick behind the afflicted person and cut it even with the top of his head, so that it will be just as long as he is tall. This stick should then be hidden in the woods where it will never be found. The same cure may also be effected by standing the ailing person against a tree, marking his height, and then boring an auger hole even with the top of his head. Next a tuft of his hair is placed in the opening, and the hole is plugged up. As soon as the person grows taller than the position of the hole, he is cured.

Mrs. Ramsey liked to talk and spoke emphatically and clearly. She was proud of the fact her "gramp" came to this country from across the waters about the time of the "Old War" (the Revolution). He had five daughters and five sons. The girls remained in Tennessee, but the boys all went to Texas. "We never did hear from them." Her father was a Gunter, her mother a Webb. Though she sold her land to the Park Commission, Mrs. Ramsey still lived on it for some years. In her garden she kept many herbs for use in making the poultices and old-fashioned remedies she described to me. She had great faith in them.

For bronchial ailments she recommended two types of poultice, one of mustard seed or another made of linsey cloth soaked in a hot mixture of mutton tallow, turpentine, camphor and lamp oil. To treat blood poisoning she applied a poultice of catnip and beadwood bark which had been boiled together. Mud from the spring, she reminded me, would cure a sprain. As a vermifuge she advised the seed from the Jerusalem oak boiled with molasses. One spoonful was the correct "doste." The "flux," that is, diarrhoea, might be relieved by a preparation compounded of sweet-gum bark and melted mutton tallow.

For a case of colic Mrs. Ramsey prescribed a tea brewed from Samson's snake root. She described the plant as having a "little, long blossom that blooms in September, a little pod, and hit blue." She depended on hulver to treat liver and stomach ailments and on dog fennel for "rheumatiz." For her, marigold had two uses, for hives and for bad colds. Catnip tea was also good "if you tuck cold," and the tops of bone set are sure "to break up the fever." "The fever" might refer to any type, pneumonia, scarlet, etc., though in this instance it was typhoid.

"A sight of people died of the fever on this branch twenty-five or thirty years ago. It began when loggin' started, and the stumps o' trees soured," giving off, according to common belief, a noxious vapor. "Elbert Carver and his son died the same day of typhoid," Mrs. Ramsey concluded.

As mentioned before, Mrs. Sutton also prescribed bone set tea for a bad cold. Mrs. Carver added, "Hit's bitterer than quinine. Hit'll kill ye or cure ye." In a case of "pneumonia fever" Aunt Rhoda Caton applied a poultice of peach tree bark and peach tree leaves. Mrs. Carver made a poultice of just peach tree bark to ease the discomfort of blisters.

Mrs. Carver relied on catnip tea "to break out the hives" and to cure colds. "Hit's also good to make ye rest and sleep good," Mrs. Crisp asserted. As a remedy for catarrh she smoked the dried stalks and leaves of catnip. For kidney and bladder trouble she used ground ivy.

Aunt Rhody Caton, at ninety years of age, was still leading an active life. On the day I came to see her, she was busy canning string beans over an open fire behind her trim two-story house, assisted by her sixty-five-year-old unmarried daughter. The two women did all the work on their small farm, tilling the fields with a hand cultivator, and planting and harvesting in season.

The kindly and efficient old lady was said to have built the fence which surrounded her property, and even to have split the rails for it. During the Civil War "the fighting went on right through Catons Grove," she told me. She smuggled clothes to the Union soldiers by carrying them beneath her dress. Once she also acted as a newsboy, by announcing to the residents of the settlement the outcome of an encounter which took place nearby.

As the mother of fourteen children, nine of whom were "a-livin' yet," she was bound to be acquainted with old-time remedies, and she readily answered my questions about them. For "the fever," she explained that bleeding was commonly practiced in the old days, adding skeptically, however, that this treatment was relied on in any unidentified ailment. In doctoring a sick baby, for example, three cuts were made under the shoulder blade. This was probably followed by "cupping," that is, drawing off the blood by suction. For croup and phthisic she often used a tea made of ground ivy, which she called "wallink."

51

Alternate remedies were a poultice made of fried onions or a brew concocted of onions and sulphur. "Roast some onions until they are soft; add to them a quantity of sulphur, and 'wrop' them in a cloth. Then squeeze out the juice, and take in doses of a teaspoonful," she recommended.

To relieve the phthisic, Elizabeth Baxter, another resident of Catons Grove, who was "in the eighty," had a prescription calling for the "biling" of camphor, turpentine, and the scales of the hickory tree. "I never knowed it to fail," she remarked. Like Aunt Rhody Caton, she advised a poultice of peach-tree bark and peach-tree leaves for "pneumonie" fever. She also used the poultice made with mustard.

Those who spend much time in the mountains will, no doubt, be interested in her simple remedy for insect bites. When one is "bee-stung" or "gnat-stung," he should "wet some tobacco and pop it right on the sting." A CCC camp physician at Smokemont, North Carolina, informed me that this application of tobacco has practical value. He said that the acid venom of the insect is counteracted by the nicotine, which is an alkali.

For "pneumonie fever," George Lemons, Gumstand, Tennessee, recommended: "Take onions and bile 'em and put 'em on your breast. You can't do nothin' better."

One of the five well-known Walker sisters of Little Greenbrier had recently recovered from a case of "pneumonie fever," when I visited them briefly at their old-fashioned log home. For a remedy her sisters put "lamp oil" (kerosene) on a woolen cloth and placed the cloth on the chest, rubbing camphorated oil on the chest to keep the lamp oil from burning. They explained, "we put the woolen cloth (on the chest) when the fever got high or when she got to smotherin'. We put it on just as hot as she could stand it." For teas efficacious against pneumonia, they employed bone set and catnip. Despite this expert care, the convalescing sister said, "I like to took a back-set when I got to knockin' about," that is, when she got on her feet again.

To cure a rattlesnake bite, the Walker sisters bathed the affected part with lamp oil, turpentine, and Roger's linament. Concerning one occasion when they used this remedy, one sister exclaimed, "You could just see the poison comin' out."

For times when a mild anesthetic was desired, they recommended "strong, hot, creamy coffee for dope."

The Walker sisters were well versed in the time-honored medical lore of the Smokies.

Some mountain words may have carried more than their apparent meaning. Of interest was the use of the word beeswax. In the Great Smoky Mountains it could mean more than the stuff of a honeycomb. If a widower said "beeswax" to a widow whom he had been "sparkin'," he was proposing marriage. If she wished to marry him, she answered "sticks."

A young "widder woman" of Indian Creek, near Bryson City, North Carolina, was courted by a man past middle age who was in fairly good circumstances. Her four children, however, not pleased with the prospect that he might become their step-father, expressed their disapproval. But the lot of a mountain woman who must raise a large family alone is not an enviable one. Hence, she said if the old "widder" (widower) declared "beeswax" again, she was going to reply "sticks."

Rainbow Falls, with a sheer drop of about seventy feet, on one of the main trails to Mt. Le Conte.

National Park Service

X

THAT'S THE WAY OLD-TIMEY FOLKS TALKED
Smokies Dialect
DISAPPEARANCE OF THE OLD SMOKIES LIFE

If there is any one thing which illustrates simply and well a people's character or group personality, it is the language they use. If their speech is a dialect of a standard language, the linguistic reflection of their personality appears in even stronger outlines than otherwise. There are colorful local or regional words, words elsewhere outmoded, but often full of pictures of folk imagery. Some of these are for articles, processes and activities which have passed out of general fashion and use. Some may be employed for rural rather than urban articles and aspects of life or vice-versa. Some may merely reflect the folk habit or way of saying things which has persisted through generations of changing urban culture. Other expressions reflective of a people's personality are proverbial comparisons; favorite phrases describing such common things as land, people, time and weather; oaths and profanity; humorous remarks; and aphorisms (or what we might call "plain observations of life").

I would like to reveal something of the life of the Smokies people by telling some of their linguistic traditions. The Smokies people and their language are practically matters of history now, for most of the area became a national park in 1934 and almost none of the original population reside within the Park boundaries now. The very few exceptions are some of the Park personnel and their families who were born and raised there, and a few families in the scenic Cades Cove who have been allowed to stay to sow the broad fields in hay and to keep their cattle in order to preserve some of the trim, agricultural neatness characteristic of this valley before the Park era. Back in 1937, when a number of elderly people had been given leases allowing them to spend the rest of their days on their old home places, Mrs. Docia Styles of Indian Creek told me about her lease. She said, "They told me I could stay as long as I lived. I told 'em that would be as long as I wanted to stay."

My studies were carried on mainly in 1937-1940, while there were still several hundred native residents in the Park. I interviewed as many of them as possible. Also I talked to and gathered information from great numbers of people who lived just beyond the boundaries of the Park, as in Gatlinburg, Emerts Cove, and on Cosby Creek. Many of these people are still living and have assisted me with my more recent collectings. Some of these people had moved down to the bordering valleys and coves when their farms and homes were bought by the Park Commission. Nevertheless, despite the people living in the fringe areas, it must be said that the old Smokies people and their life are things of the past. The few old-timers still alive have merged their ways of living in the customs of the less mountainous, more accessible countryside and towns roundabout. Besides, for people everywhere— in towns and cities, in the Southern Appalachians generally, on the prairies of Missouri and Nebraska, on isolated farms and ranches of the Far West, times have changed. A series of general social changes has been brought about for everybody by such things as the automobile, the movies, radio, television, the wars with their radical displacement of life, national shifts in the political picture, increasing industrialization, the world uneasiness over the possibility of atomic warfare, etc.

Into the Smokies region, besides the Park itself, have come the gigantic Tennessee Valley Authority and the huge atomic energy plant at Oak Ridge. The TVA filled wide, fertile valleys with lakes for producing power, displaced large rural settlements (with accompanying social and human pains), provided thousands of new jobs and opportunities, and in general revolutionized life in areas of the South far distant from East Tennessee. Added to these disruptive forces was the Manhattan Engineering District at Oak Ridge, which during World War II created a community of 75,000 people, intermingling residents of the Tennessee Valley with people from all over the country.

Some of these changes have been humanly illustrated by North Callahan in his American Folkways book *Smoky Mountain Country* (N. Y., 1952). This author tells (p. 176) of a bootlegger who, living in contentment in the Smokies, operated his still beside a creek when all the land round about was bought for the new national park.

"The 'legger' had to move. He went to Union County, where he resumed his occupation of making moonshine. After being here a few years, the TVA moved in and took his land for the Norris Dam basin. He next moved down on the Clinch River, and there was again engaged in his favorite vocation when the Oak Ridge project came along. This was the last straw.

"Used to be, the only federal men I dealt with was the revenoors," he snorted, "and we understood each other. Now it seems that every time I come home from a run, they's a guvermint man a-settin' on my doorstep with papers orderin' me to move. Ef I knowed of a place where there weren't no guvermint men but revenoors, I'd shore go there."

Of the changes wrought by TVA he says (pp. 177-178):

"First of all, it brought electric power where it had never been available before. Probably next in importance was the cheap fertilizer it provided farmers."

In sum, we have a picture of two to three million tourists soaking up the beauties of the area every year, industrialization springing up

The author on a field trip to Cove Creek recording mountain folk songs. Singers Zeb and Winfred Hannah are in the background.

throughout the whole region, "furriners" from all over working and settling there, and improved standards of living. There are also increased education and (through the county bookmobiles) increased reading of books, and general modernization of living. As a consequence, there has been rapid elimination of the colorful aspects of old Smokies life, including their hearty, rugged, and picturesque dialect.

But as interesting as is the subject of social living in transition, it is not the present subject of discussion. My purpose in giving some of these details was to show how life in the Tennessee and North Carolina Appalachians is becoming radically changed, and to contrast with the flux of modern conditions the much more static, frontierlike conditions which prevailed in life and language before civilization and industry came to the mountains.

VOCABULARY

It is impossible to characterize the old Smokies speech by giving a few isolated words; abundant examples of syntax, rhythmic and intonation patterns, and idioms, as well as an extensive vocabulary, are required to illustrate the nature of this mountain dialect. However, the vocabulary—the words which people employed in everyday life—does show something about the life of the speakers, their interests, concerns, and imagination.

Some of the interesting terms apply to *topography*:

BALD: a treeless mountain top characteristic of the Smokies, as in Bearwallow Bald.

BALSAM: a mountain top in the Balsam Mountains, as in Cataloochee Balsam.

BENCH: a level area, sometimes cultivated, on the side of a mountain.

BRANCH: a small stream, as in Woolly Tops Branch.

BUTT: the abrupt end of a mountain ridge, as in Mollies Butt, at the end of Mollies Ridge.

COVE: a widening out of a mountain valley, or a meadow land between mountains, as in Cades Cove, Emerts Cove.

DEADENING: an area where the trees have been killed by girdling (in order to clear land for farming).

DRAIN (nearly always pronounced *dreen*): a small spring with little water, on a mountain side or in a little hollow.

FORK AND PRONG: important tributaries of a creek or river as in Ravens Fork, Kephart Prong.

FITIFIED: as in Fitified Springs: an intermittent spring.

GAP: a depression on a ridge, as in Newfound Gap.

HOLLOW (pronounced holler): a small valley, as in Pretty Hollow.

KNOB: a mountain top, as in Brier Knob, Lufty Knob.

LEAD: a long ridge, usually extending from a higher ridge, as in Twenty Mile Lead.

Uncle George Lemons of the Gumstand, near Gatlinburg, liked his bees.

NEW GROUND: land newly cleared, for tilling.

RUN: a marshy place or small stream, as in Tight Run, near Ravensford.

SCALD: a bare hillside; sometimes FIRE SCALD when the hill has been denuded of growth by fire.

SWAG: a depression on a ridge, as in Big Swag, or Round Mountain Ridge.

TOP: a mountain top, as in Rocky Top.

YELLOW PATCH: a burned-over area grown up with thick brush.

A number of terms refer to the dense, impenetrable rhododendron thickets so characteristic of the Smokies and the adjacent mountains: laurel bed, lettuce bed, rough, slick, woolly (as in woolly head, woolly ridge, woolly top, yellow patch, and hell (as in Huggins Hell).

Perusal of the United States Geographical Survey map of the Park provides a fascinating study of Great Smokies place names.

Some words apply to *home construction,* like:

CHIMLEY: a fireplace.

CHINKIN': sticks and mud used to stop up cracks between logs.

COMB: the ridge pole of the roof.

DAUBIN': mud used as plaster for a chimney.

FIREBOARD: the mantel of a fireplace.

GALLERY: porch (very old-fashioned even in the mountains).

KIVER (cover): roof (said to be obsolete).

PUNCHEON: a halved log used in constructing the floor.

A more modern expression is "boxed house," for a house with outside walls built of vertically set planks, with strips nailed on to cover the cracks between boards.

Some words refer to *old utensils* and *implements* used or made on the mountain farm:

BAKER, OVEN, OR DUTCH OVENS: a cast iron pan with three legs and a cover set in the coals of the fireplace.

BEE-GUM: bee-hive (made from a section of a gum tree).

GRITTER: a grater for making grits.

PIGGIN: a small wooden bucket or churn.

Some words represent *social work activities* (called "bees" in some parts of the country):

BEAN-STRINGIN': a group of women, or of girls with their sweethearts, putting beans on strings to make "leather britches" (also called "shuck beans," that is, dried beans).

CORN-SHUCKIN': a festive occasion for shucking corn.

HAY-THRASHIN': a cooperative job of thrashing hay to obtain grain or seeds.

HOUSE-RAISIN': a community gathering for assisting a neighbor in erecting a house.

LOG-ROLLIN: clearing an area of logs for home construction and farming.

QUILTIN': an assemblage of women to help a woman make quilts. Some of the words refer to *foods* of the mountain farm, like:

CAT HEADS: biscuits.

CORN PONE: a flat loaf of corn bread.

CRACKLINGS: the crisp roasted or fried skin or rind of pork or bacon; also the edible fat trimmings of the entrails of a hog from which lard is rendered.

FRUIT: (as in West Virginia) at the table usually refers to stewed apples: "Have some of the fruit."

GARDEN SASS or GARDEN SALLET: fresh vegetables grown in a garden. According to Mrs. Wesley Metcalf, Del Rio, Tennessee, mustard, turnip, or wild greens were also called "sallet."

GRITS: corn (sometimes fresh) grated in a gritter.

GRITTED BREAD: corn bread made of gritted meal.

HOE CAKE: a large flat cake of bread made of corn meal, water, and salt, usually baked in a "hoe cake baker" (Dutch oven). Apparently so-called because it was made on the blade of a hoe in the fireplace.

KROUT: Sauerkraut.

LEATHER BRITCHES: beans dried in the pod, "then biled hull and all."

LIVER PUDDING or LIVER MUSH: According to Mrs. Wesley Metcalf, Del Rio, Tennessee, and Mrs. Fannie Stinnett, Waynesville, North Carolina, liver pudding consists of boiled hog's liver or cow's liver and sometimes portions of pork (usually the pig's head) mixed with corn meal, water, sage, salt and pepper. Sometimes it is allowed to harden, when it may be sliced and fried. (This, incidentally, is a very tasty dish.)

MIDDLIN' OF BACON: "side meat" or side of bacon.

RED-EYE GRAVY: is made by "burning" a little ham or sausage in a frying pan, allowing the red juice to come out; then adding flour, red pepper and water.

ROASTIN' EARS: corn on the cob.

SWEETENIN': sugar, honey, or molasses.

WHITE SOP: chicken gravy or other white gravy made with unbrowned flour.

Some terms apply to *illnesses*:

BACK-SET: a relapse.

BUCK-AGGERS: chills and fever.

CROUP: a cough.

THE FEVER: typhoid fever, usually.

HARD FIT: a severe epileptic fit.

JANDERS: jaundice.

LIQUOR PELLAGRY: a skin infection due to diet deficiency in turn induced by excessive drinking.

60

PHTHISIC: asthma.

PNEUMONIE FEVER: pneumonia.

SETTIN' UP WITH THE SICK: sitting up to minister to the sick and keep them company.

A number of words refer to *hunting* and *trapping*:

BEAR PEN: a dead-fall bear trap.

BEEF SHOOTS: shooting matches in which the prize is a steer, which is driven off on foot.

COLD TRAIL: an animal trail on which the scent has grown faint.

COLD TRAILER: a dog which can pick up or follow a cold trail.

HIGH POWER: a high-power gun.

HOG RIFLE: an old-fashioned, home-made cap-and-ball rifle for hunting.

PLOTT HOUND: a strong, rugged bear hound locally bred by the Plott family.

RIFLE GUN: a gun in which the bore has been grooved or rifled.

TREE IN A CLIFT: to drive an animal onto a cliff or into a hole in a cliff.

TREE IN THE GROUND: to drive an animal into a hole in the ground.

TURKEY PEN: a trap or cage into which wild turkeys are lured by grains of corn leading to the enclosure.

VARMENT: a wild animal. Varments are explained as being "bears, wild cats, and things like that."

Some words refer to *old customs* like:

HARP SINGIN': a community or church singing in which a *Sacred Harp* song book is used. (*The Sacred Harp* is a collection of psalm and hymn tunes with the music written with shape notes.)

HOE-DOWN: a boisterous square dance, or "frolic" (as it is also locally called).

INFARE: refers to when the newly married couple go to their own or the bridegroom's home.

PROTRACTIVE MEETIN': a series of revival services continued for a week or two.

SERENADE: "a shivaree" or celebration after a wedding; also the noisy merriment of the night before Christmas, consisting of going from house to house, shooting guns, ringing cowbells, or the like.

SETTIN' UP WITH THE SICK

WAKE: settin' up with the corpse.

It is obvious that practically all these terms are old-fashioned expressions that at some time or other may have been used over much of the country, especially on the ever-moving frontier, but that survived later in remote and inaccessible areas. Such places are called relic areas. Possibly relatively few of those mentioned and others not mentioned are limited largely to Southern usage: bald, bee-gum, corn pone, evenin' (afternoon), grits, gritter, ha'nt (ghost), leather britches, pone of bread (a loaf of corn bread), rough (a thicket), roastin' ears. Perhaps only a very small number are restricted to the Smokies and adjacent areas because the phenomenon referred to is more or less localized: hell, slick, woolly (as in woolly head), yaller patch, for the impassable rhododendron thickets. But one can never be sure; people bring most of their expressions ·with them and carry them from one place to another as they move about the country.

However, these words and others like them indicate the concerns and occupations of the Smokies people, and suggest that they retained their frontier interests, names for things, and ways down to recent times.

COMPARISONS AND FIGURES OF SPEECH

Proverbial comparisons and similes, because they appeal to the imagination or desire for novelty, are likely to spring up at any time and may travel far and wide; and some of the same expressions can be found almost any place in the country. But still a collection of them may have much local color and reflect the local personality. Some that I gathered in the Great Smokies are:

AS BAD AS THE DEVIL AND TOM WALKER (probably suggested by the legend recorded by Washington Irving and others).

AS BROKE AS A CONVICT.

AS CLEAN AS A HOUND'S TOOTH.

AS CROSS AS A SORE-TAILED BEAR.

AS DEAD AS FOUR O'CLOCK: "He killed the bear dead as four o'clock." Also "deader'n four o'clock." Is it possible that this phrase is connected with the four o'clock plant, one of the nightshades, which is said to have been used, broken up in milk, as a fly poison? . But more probably it refers to the hours of the dead, when ghosts walk, especially between midnight and dawn. This simile reminds us of the common saying "the dead of night" and Shakespeare's lines in *The Rape of Lucrece*:

> Now stole upon the time the dead of night
>
> . . . .
>
> No comfortable star did lend his light,
> No noise but owls' and wolves' death-boding cries.

AS DIRTY AS A HAWG.

AS DRUNK AS A BILED OWL.

AS FAST AS SNYDER'S HOUSE CAT or AS SNYDER'S PUP.

AS HAPPY AS A COON.

AS HAPPY AS A DEAD PIG IN THE SUNSHINE.

AS ILL (ill-tempered) AS A HORNET: "That teacher was ill as a hornet."

AS MAD AS A WET HEN.

AS MAD AS WHIZ.

AS MEAN AS A BLACK SNAKE, or AS STRIPED SNAKES.

AS PLAIN AS A SHOE: "He's a millionaire, but you would never know it. He's as plain as a shoe."

AS PRETTY AS A SPECKLED PUP UNDER A LITTLE RED WAGON.

AS ROUGH AS A HACKLE (a comb for removing the coarse parts of hemp).

AS STRAIGHT AS A MARTEN TO HIS (HER) GOURD (NEST).

AS TIGHT AS DICK'S HATBAND.

AS TOUGH AS A PIGGING STRING (said to be a rawhide string often used in tying the legs of a pig together before carrying it.

AS TOUGH AS A PINE KNOT.

AS UGLY AS A MUD FENCE DAUBEP WITH TADPOLES.

AS WELCOME AS THE FLOWERS IN MAY.

Similar expressions (employing *like*) are:

TO TAKE OFF LIKE A SCALDED DOG or LIKE SNYDER'S PUP.

TO SCROUGE OVER LIKE YOU HAD A FAMILY.

In trying to find a man in the Walland Creek section, I asked a boy what he looked like. He replied, "Like a skeerd hant (ghost), I reckon." Uncle Mitch Sutton of Gnat Camp, near Mt. Sterling, said, "Old man Andy just looked like a forked stick with some britches on it." Frank Lambert, of Tow String Creek, who is a sixteenth Cherokee Indian and has just enough Indian blood to be allowed to live on the Qualla Indian Reservation (adjoining the Park), told on a phonograph disc of a hunt in which he and his hunting companions fell in the creek on a very cold morning. He said, "Our britches legs was froze so you could feel the ice. They rattled just like tin." In asking someone on a couch or porch swing to move over to make room for others, one could say, "Scrouge over like you had a family." Of a stubborn person one hears, "He had a head like Collins' ram." Not very complimentary but apt is the saying, "He looked as sneaky as a sheep-killing dog," and one recognizes certain descriptive truth in "Her tongue was goin' like a bell clapper."

A story is told about Uncle Tobe Phillips, locally famed as a hunter and a "character," one of whose exploits was described above. Tobe had had a falling out with his wife who left him for a time and returned to her "people." When she returned, he was so glad to see her he said, "You look like a star that fell from heaven."

Other common sayings employ the pattern "like the farmer's old mule":

LIKE THE FARMER'S OLD MULE, HE JUST DON'T GIVE A DAMN.

A hunter told me, "That bobcat was squallin' just like somebody."

Other comparative expressions are:

HE KILLED HIM (a bear) DEADER'N FOUR O'CLOCK. (Cf. dead as four o'clock.)

63

WE ALL HAVE MORE TIME THAN MONEY.

AINT' THAT ONE MORE SIGHT!

When I met Neil Phillips of Muddy Holler, near Newport, Tennessee, and asked him in an interview how old he was, he answered, "I'm older than good." Later, in referring to his little grand-daughter who was playing in the yard in front of the porch where we were talking, he said, "She ain't bigger'n a cricket much." Jake Welch, of Hazel Creek, in telling on a disc of the good times he had before the Park came in, exclaimed, "God, we had one more time in this world a-bear-huntin'!" Of one indefatigable story teller, a Roaring Fork man said, "He can tell more tales than John (referring to the Biblical John) told on the Isle of Patmos."

Some typical superlative expressions often heard are:

THE BEST TICKLED I EVER WAS.

THAT WAS THE WORST EVER I WAS SCARED.

HE WAS THE CRABBEDEST OLD FELLER EVER I SEED.

HE TOLD SOME OF THE MASTEREST STORIES: A BODY COULDN'T HARDLY BELIEVE THEM.

TOM BARNES WAS THE COMPLETEST HUNTER I WAS EVER ACQUAINTED WITH.

Major Woody of Cataloochee, as was mentioned above, chafing under the prohibition against hunting in the Park, complained, "The wust, sorriest things they is like bob cats, you cain't kill."

Of similar picturesque effect are certain popular *could* and *would* expressions which are a kind of "tall talk":

HIT (a pig) COULD EAT THE GUTS OUT OF A PUNKIN THROUGH A HOLE IN THE FENCE, ITS NOSE WAS SO LONG!

HE WOULD STEAL THE HAT OFF YOUR HEAD, AND YOU A-LOOKIN' AT HIM.

HE WOULD STEAL A CHEW OF TOBACCO OUT OF YOUR MOUTH IF YOU OPENED YOUR MOUTH TO YAWN.

YOU COULDN'T TOUCH HIM WITH A TEN-FOOT POLE.

HE COULD A FIT A CIRCLE SAWMILL.

Also common is "that feller would fight a circle saw."

Also very familiar are sayings like "I was so tough I could crack chestnut burrs with my heel," and the uncomplimentary "His head is full of stump water" (that is, he is stupid), "He ain't got the brains of a sap sucker."

A more direct imagery is found in a number of metaphorical words and phrases:

CAPTAIN: One who excels.

CATTY: active. "He's a catty old feller."

CLEAN SOMEONE'S PLOW: to lick or punish: "I'll clean your plow (for that)" is a common warning to unruly children or other malefactors.

DEVIL'S KITCHEN: one woman's term for her husband's stillhouse (Aden Carver).

TO FOUNDER: to eat too much. "Don't get foundered at that Democratic barbecue" was said ironically in view of the small portions of food served.

GENERATION OF CHILDREN: a large family of children.

GENTLEMAN: an animal one is shooting at, said humorously.

TO GET THE DEADWOOD ON SOMEONE: to learn something about someone which he doesn't want people·to know.   A man can be pretty nice if you "have the deadwood on him."

TO GIVE SOMEONE THE EYE: to show someone romantic interest.

TO GROUND HOG IT: to live in the poorest circumstances.

HEADACHE OR TOOTHACHE MEDICINE: liquor (veiled meaning).

TO JUMP THE BROOM: to get married, referring to an old protection against witches.   As reported in Harry M. Hyatt, *Folklore from Adams County Illinois* (New York, 1935), p. 372: "Let a bride jump over a broom just before she goes into her new home and she will never be 'hoodooed' there."   Mrs. Polly Grooms, of Newport, Tennessee, said, "Lay a broom across the door, and no witches won't step over that, they say."

POPSKULL: rotgut whiskey.

PUT YOUR MONEY WHERE YOUR MOUTH IS: "put up or shut up," which is also used.

A ROUGH OLD COON: a hardbitten, aggressive old man; a hard fighter.

Mr. George Lemons, of the Gumstand, told of General Morgan during the Civil War.   He said, "He was a rough old coon.   He made it in his mind to never surrender.   He could a fit a circle sawmill."

Of someone with a large family, one may hear, "He has a whole house full of children."   Concerning Quill Rose, who was a famous character of Eagle Creek and a well-known moonshiner, someone said, "I'll bet he has drunk this whole house full of liquor."

"Popskull" is the name for low-grade moonshine, a term now being replaced by the expressions "gray cloud" and "silver cloud," with reference to the "galvanize" (zinc) corroded from the steel still by the acid of the mash.

"Watchin' his bees" or "waitin' for his bees to swarm" are euphemisms for expecting a baby: "John, when are your bees going to swarm?"

THE COLORFUL SPEECH OF HUNTERS

Stories and incidents told by hunters are usually striking because of their rugged, imaginative turns of phrase.

"Let me just blaze that gentleman (animal) by the right of the ear," said Ashley Moore, of Walkers Valley, raising his hog rifle (fashioned with primitive tools by a local artisan, but, like most such home-made firearms, accurate and powerful). He pretended to take aim as in the good old days, and then went on to tell of an incident at a hunting campfire:

"A pant'er was attracted by frying venison.
In a thought or two it came out and screamed.
Wouldn't come up within shine of the fire."

By "the shine of the fire" is meant the reflection of light in the animal's eyes, making him a target at night. The eyes of many animals reflect light.

A "bear fight" is a fight between the dogs and a bear, or with the dogs baying and badgering it while the hunter waits for a chance to kill it without shooting a dog. In a "bear race" the dogs try to catch up with the bear and corner it against a tree or a cliff. They try to "hem the bear," as the mountaineer says. Often the bear "trees" (climbs a tree), whereupon the hunter shoots it down. When the bear hounds "hem the bear," the bear in its rage and frustration often "grits" or "pops" its teeth. Uncle Tom Barnes of Cove Creek and Big Creek once killed a bear with a knife. The story of this incident is repeated here, this time in the actual words of the narrator, his son Bill Barnes—partly for its unusual dramatic effect, but especially because of its simple but vivid imagery. (It was phonographically recorded in 1939, two years after the original account given above):

"My father was drivin' some cattle . . . an' he come up to a party had been fightin' a bear with dogs, an' it was eaten' up their dogs in a laurel bed. He axed the party fer a gun to go down an' kill that bear. An' there wasn't a man that had loaded powder or a loaded gun. He couldn't get anything to kill it with. An' it was just eatin' their dogs up . . . An' he run up an' stobbed his knife into it an' cut a big long gash plumb to the holler of the bear. An' the bear wheeled on 'im an' he said it 'peared like he could feel it a-bitin' 'im nearly. He could hear it poppin' its teeth . . . He took a run-ago 'an run his arm into that hole he cut into it, an' run it right up about his heart an' give it a yank or two, an' that bear sunk down an' bawled, he said, like a calf."

PICTURESQUE SAYINGS OF WEATHER AND TIME

Expressions of weather and time are always favorites with us, and so they have been in the Great Smokies. Newt Ownby of Elkmont, telling how a man got lost one time, explained, "The fog shut down on the mountain and he couldn't see to travel."

Zeb Crisp, of Hazel Creek, telling how he got caught in a storm while herding cattle on top of Smoky, said, "Just about dusky dark it was snowing like water pourin' out of a bucket."

Mrs. Bill Brown, of Ravensford, suggested the winter beauty of a mountain forest: "Hit's the pertiest sight in the world when the snow covers these trees and you can see their shapes."

Old Dave Sparks of Cades Cove explained that the snowfall in the cove was light whereas it was heavy in the mountains roundabout: "Snow is shoe-mouth deep in the cove when it's knee-deep in the mountains."

When hunters tree a raccoon, they sometimes have to cut the tree down to get the animal. Frank Lambert, of Tow String Creek, said: "Time we got the tree cut down it was just a-breakin' daylight."

During a heavy rain one day in early summer, Sherman Meyers of Cades Cove said, "You can hear the corn grow."

Weather often means bad weather, a rain or snow storm: "We're goin' to have some weather." Or one may hear: "There's no need of you goin' out, it's so weathery." One way of explaining the phenomenon of snow is as follows: "The Devil's whippin' his wife and all her feathers are comin' out," which has some interesting connections in folklore.

Fonze Cable, an old bear hunter of Cades Cove and Thunderhead, told how a bear almost got away from his party in a snowstorm: "He shot two shoots with the automatic pistol and he hit him in the bottom of the foot. The bear run on and the snow a-bilin' and the dogs a-fightin' . . ."

One summer day in Cades Cove, a local resident and his wife took me to the site of the old family home. The building had been removed by the National Park Service, and the ground was overgrown with bushes and trees. But the old spring and some strawberry vines were still there. "I reckon that spring's worth a thousand dollars!" exclaimed Mrs. Myers, with a feeling for her old home which only a displaced mountaineer may know. We enjoyed ourselves resting under the shade of trees and picking strawberries. There was a rumble of thunder on Gregory's Bald overhead. "I reckon we'd orta be goin'," Mrs. Myers said. "Hit's lookin' a little rainy and the clouds are a-bilin' on them mountains."

And while the clouds are a-bilin' on the Smokies, I reckon I'd orta be goin' too.

Clouds over Cades Cove.   National Park Service

ACKNOWLEDGMENTS

National Park Service officials, Great Smokies friends, and other friends have been generous with assistance in the preparation of this booklet. Roy E. Appleman, formerly Historian in the National Park Service, and Dr. Ronald F. Lee, now Regional Director, Region Five, National Park Service, made it possible for me to conduct my linguistic and folklore research in the mountains through an appointment as Collaborator. Dr. Lee subsequently honored me with several brief appointments. Arthur Stupka, Park Naturalist, assisted constantly with suggestions, contacts, and equipment. I thank Columbia University for the kindness of financial aid, guidance, and inspiration, particularly my distinguished teachers, Cabell Greet and the late Harry Morgan Ayres.

Gratitude without measure is due also to the many mountain people and residents who kindly gave me information. Besides those mentioned herein were Lewis Clabo, Glenn Newman, Ellis Ogle, Amos Reagan, Louis Reagan, and Audely Whaley, Gatlinburg; Jack Johnson, Townsend; the William Shults family, particularly Glen Shults, Emerts Cove; Laura Hance, Burl McGaha, Phoebe Ramsey, and Lee Webb, Newport; the Wesley Metcalf family, particularly the beloved "Aunt Lou," Wilford, and Fred, Del Rio; Mack Caldwell, Sam Leatherwood, and "Uncle Mitch" Sutton, Mount Sterling; the Will Palmers and "Uncle Steve" Woody, Cataloochee; Fay Leatherwood, Carl, Brown, and Bessie Messer, and Robert and Teague Williams, White Oak, Haywood County; the Glenn Nolands of Upper Crabtree Creek; Flora Medford, Iron Duff; William Moore, Saunook; W. C. Medford, Taylor Sutton, H. C. Wilburn, and Jonathan Woody, Waynesville. The Metcalfs and the Messers were always most "free-hearted" with both information and traditional mountain hospitality; I have spent many pleasant days with these good friends. There were unforgettable trips to almost inaccessible mountain homes with W. C. Medford and the Nolands. Jonathan Woody has extended various generous courtesies. The contributions of many others will be acknowledged if and when booklets containing their accounts are written.

Former mountain residents have proved to be excellent sources of recollected lore. I wish to thank Lena Leatherwood Fowler, formerly of Mount Sterling, now in California, for countless details and for her prolonged interest in this project; Lola Oliver Hammond, formerly of

Franklin, North Carolina, and Tellico Plains, Tennessee, now in California, for some unusual expressions and sayings; J. Lacy Barnes, Knoxville, for further details about his father, Bill Barnes, and others; and Vernon Metcalf, Department of Public Welfare, State of Tennessee, for reading all the copy and improving the accuracy.

Still other friends have helped in revising the manuscript, or have contributed their knowledge or talents in other ways. I wish to acknowledge with gratitude the assistance of: Mary Sue Guthrie for typing; Helen Hinckley for arrangement of materials; Virginia Alexander for typing; my colleagues at Pasadena City College, California, Walter Bennett for various favors and advice on printing, and Frank Hammond for practical help; Joseph A. Sharp, Rule High School, Knoxville, for recent pleasant interviews with mountain people to obtain accuracy on several important issues; Louise Padelford, Sondley Library, Asheville, for suggestions on style; George Myers Stephens for encouragement and illustrations; National Park Service personnel for additional great help — John O. Morrell for verifications, Mary Ruth Chiles for devoted concern in selecting illustrations, and especially Park Naturalist Arthur Stupka for conscientious interest in the study at all stages, from research to print; Mary Hartshorn for careful editing; Gladys Snyder for invaluable guidance and assistance in readying the manuscript, proofreading, and illustrating. Any shortcomings and oversights, however, are not due to my friends and assistants; they are my charge alone.

To all who assisted me I express hearty and sincere thanks.

Mountain Laurel.

INDEX

The Chandler Jenkins house, with pig pen and worm fence, Indian Camp Creek.

INDEX

The old one-roomed Lequire House, Cades Cove.

INDEX

Mt. LeConte with its approaches are covered with a stately balsam forest. National Park Service